Addicted To Certainty

Addicted To Certainty

The Journey From A Cultural Cosmology To A Spiritual Cosmology

E. Jack Lemon MDiv. CSW

Note for Librarians: A cataloguing record for this book is available from Library and Archives Canada at www.collectionscanada.ca/amicus/index-e.html
ISBN 1-4120-9036-9

Book cover designed by Kimberlee J. Cinko
kimmijo@mac.com

Illustration by Ann Savory

Printed in Victoria, BC, Canada. Printed on paper with minimum 30% recycled fibre. Trafford's print shop runs on "green energy" from solar, wind and other environmentally-friendly power sources.

TRAFFORD
PUBLISHING™
Offices in Canada, USA, Ireland and UK

Book sales for North America and international:
Trafford Publishing, 6E–2333 Government St.,
Victoria, BC V8T 4P4 CANADA
phone 250 383 6864 (toll-free 1 888 232 4444)
fax 250 383 6804; email to orders@trafford.com
Book sales in Europe:
Trafford Publishing (UK) Limited, 9 Park End Street, 2nd Floor
Oxford, UK OX1 1HH UNITED KINGDOM
phone 44 (0)1865 722 113 (local rate 0845 230 9601)
facsimile 44 (0)1865 722 868; info.uk@trafford.com
Order online at:
trafford.com/06-0792

10 9 8 7 6 5 4 3

*This book is dedicated
with gratitude to*
Grandfather

The Cover

The artwork on the cover of the book is a Vibrational Energy Painting. The medium is artist ink on deer hide, accented with Floridian red sand and pipe ash. The painting is titled, "I Am Thee, My Journey from the Cultural Cosmology to My Spiritual Cosmology."

The Cover Artist's Story

Dear Reader,

The title of this painting expresses my core truth. My journey has been similar to your own. I had a difficult childhood, lost my first husband after nine years of marriage. Now I am remarried to a wonderful man. I have four children, three stepchildren, and 13 grandchildren.

I have sought for most of my life to find a way to have peace. It has also been my path as an artist to create out of both joy and pain. I believed inspiration came from the tension between these two opposites. I did not know that profound inspiration could emerge from reality itself. I assumed for most of my life that what I experienced was real. It was not until I went through the process that Jack teaches that I finally experienced true reality.

True reality is rooted in my knowing that I exist. With that as a solid base, I am now able not only to experience but also to express the deep power that I find in knowings. I recommend you read this book and go through the experience of finding your core truth. It has opened my life and set me on paths that were always blocked by me before.

Love,
Joyce Staelgraeve
Artist in residence
Many Forks Retreat Center

"All these things I have done you can do,
even greater things than I have done you can do"
Jesus

"Don't study the Buddha, become the Buddha"
Wayne

"The more one grows to know oneself,
the more one can grow to know
God and the world."
E. Jack Lemon

Contents

Acknowledgements and Thanks

To my daughter, Renee, for finding a place for me to pray on our way back from the ocean. That experience started this stage of my journey.

To my beloved wife and editor, Donna, and her gross of red pens. How do you acknowledge someone like your wife, who is so much a part of you that at times you seem to share the same reality, as well as the same home?

To Ann, for her support, editing and laughter.

To Kim and Scott for their tough critiques and support.

To Joyce and Rich for the use of their cottage for writing and for their belief in me.

To Sherry for her invaluable technical support.

To Meri-Lynn for where you have been, are, and will be.

To Lynn and Paul for their quiet love and support.

To Dee for designing the webpage and for your subtle creativity.

To my people and church members for their patience and support.

Most of all, to the energy and peace of Bear Creek Farm.

Forward

Before we begin, I would like to share with you my perspective about the purpose of this book and the history of the teachings.

What I will be sharing with you in the book is not my truth, rather it is a process by which you can discover and experience your own truth. That experience of truth is reality* for you.

The above statement is quite literally true; it has been my experience that "the truth† that will set you free" is not a truth that is a sincere belief, but truth that is reality.

I know that this experience of reality is unmistakable and equally indefinable to any other person. We can share, however, with each other the journey and joy we experience when we discover reality in the present moment.

Reality is defined as what truly is. The closest we as humans can get to knowing "what is" is our personal perspective of it. This perspective, that all we can know and experience about reality is by definition, personal and subjective, allows us to be free of debilitating fear, overwhelming guilt, and unreasonable anger. We can view others and ourselves without judgment. Our past and future no longer share the same reality as our interactions in the present. In other words, we can choose to live our lives with as much joy and success as we desire.

---

*Reality is a state of self-evident existence. Reality does not need anything else to validate that it exists. Hence, the definition of reality is that it is. Perceived reality is the interpretation of reality.
†Truth is what you sincerely believe is complete and accurate.

13

This statement is not an advertisement for the latest and greatest self-help technique. It is a about the way we are designed to live. You do not need to have faith to live in this fashion. You just need a mind that is willing to think, courage to explore new thoughts, and a willingness to work at seeing reality.

If you are sufficiently happy with your life and are experiencing an appropriate amount of success, then there is probably no reason for you to read this book. The reason for this is simple. Reality, as you are experiencing it, is acceptable.

I have been an ordained clergy since 1973 and a licensed psychotherapist since 1980. Most of my life, I have been looking for a way to experience truth, God, and the depth of love. In other words, I wanted peace in my everyday life. I believed it was possible but could not find it.

I followed two paths in trying to find peace. These were by inclination and training a theological journey through the church and a psychotherapeutic trail through the body/mind.

The difficulty I had with the theological approach was its implication that my mind was not important. I was taught that what I needed was faith, which was to be found in my heart. Prayer was not a process of the mind, but rather the experience of silencing the mind so that the heart could speak.

Since I was a child, it never made any sense to me that the Creator/God would give me this gift of a mind, and then want me not to use it or possibly remove/ignore it so that I could effectively encounter him.

I have discovered that I can use my mind to experience and interact with Spirit. I can rationally know and experience that I belong "in" the Living Spirit of Life.

The difficulty I had with the psychological/ therapeutic approach to life was that it did not seem to work. It did not matter how many issues I resolved, how rational my thinking processes were, or ultimately how effective my self-talk was; the peace I sought eluded me. In the end, I discovered that both approaches, the religious and the therapeutic, are halves of the same whole. When I used perspectives from both approaches, I discovered a way to experience peace in my everyday life.

So, what is this book about? All of you know the story of the ugly duckling. This book shows you what happened in order for the ugly duckling to become a swan. This book will teach you concepts and skills which enable you not to change reality, but to change your experience of it. It will show you how you can grow from where you are now to where you always have been. This is not a misprint or a riddle. Magic is only magic until you know how it is done. What I teach is how to discover who you really are and, therefore, always have been. I can help you discover how to develop into what you want to be. The real secret is that only you can know who you are. I can teach you how to find you.

The journey of the "I" to find itself, can only begin when it is unsatisfied. The truth of the old saying that "you cannot know what you want until you discovered what you do not want," is accurate. Its accuracy can only be recognized through experience, specifically your experience.

In my years as a minister and as a therapist, my people and clients have taught me many things. It may be that one of the most important things I have learned is individuals see, hear, and feel the world differently.

It is important that you, the reader, understand that there is a journey of the *self**, learning to become aware of itself (self-awareness). I have told the story of the journey from its beginning to its present stage in four different styles. These styles reflect four different ways that people can view the world. There are many more than these four, but these are the ones I am most familiar with.

It has been my experience, not only personally but also with my clients and parishioners, that what I have to share is life changing and powerful. I know it is powerful because of their change in behavior and their outlook on life.

It is empowering anyone to know with certainty that he is in charge of his world. This perspective gives you the freedom to be yourself. Because of this, you are free to live in the world without trying to control it or being controlled by it. You are no longer a victim and are free to experience loving yourself.

One other thing I should mention, you will read throughout the book references to God/Creator/Spirit. You will also notice that often when I refer to God/Creator/Spirit, I use the word, "he." My experience with God/ Creator/ Spirit, has led me to know that God/Creator/Spirit, is not gender specific.

Rationally this makes, sense, since "he" is the creator and sustainer of all things, all things are apart of "him." Most aspects of creation are not gender specific. Are there male and female stars? What about wind, or

---

* The self is the identification and nature of a person. The specific definition of the self depends on which cosmological perspective one uses to view oneself.
In the Cultural cosmology, the self is defined as if it were substance, separate and distinct from the universe.
In the Spiritual cosmology, the self only exists in the "moment" and cannot be separated from the universe.

rain? I believe that God/ Creator/ Spirit, cannot be limited and in fact just is.

Now as to why I keep referring to God/ Creator/ Spirit, as him or he, the reason is simple. I am married and have been married for 25 years to a lady who has been an English Teacher for 29 years. She told me that it is grammatically correct and proper to use "he" when referring to anything that is not gender specific.

I do not know about you, but I learned in the 10th grade not to argue with an English teacher. In addition, 25 years of marriage to one of the most dedicated teachers I know, has taught me not to argue with my wife on this subject. So if you are unhappy with my seemingly gender specific language please take it up with My Lady. I am staying out of this argument.

I truly wish you Peace, Shalom, and the Peace of the Pipe. All are the same prayer, my prayer for you, that you find the Peace that passes all understanding.

Namaste
Jack

Why You Want To Read This Book

I believe that you want to read this book for the following reasons:

- You are dissatisfied with your life thus far.
- Your life has become so complex that you are not sure what is real anymore.
- You have important questions but you have not been able to find answers to them.
- You wonder as you look at your life,
    "If this is all there is."
- You do not know who you are.
- You wonder whether a creator exists and cares.

The list of reasons why you want to read this book in many ways is endless. It may be that the simplest way to express what I believe is the underlying issue for all of the reasons is to say, "You are no longer certain, what *works for you.*" You have tried many different ways to make sense of the world, but you and the world keep repeating the same patterns. What I teach is how to identify those patterns, and then remove them.

One of the annoying aspects of living in our complex world is that you have simple questions but are unable to find definitive answers. What I mean by definitive is answers that are real and make sense to you.

Here are examples of some "unanswerable questions" that at I have gathered from clients.

- Why have I not experienced God's forgiving me?
- How can I get over a past trauma, when I feel the same way today as I did when it happened?

- What can I do? I feel trapped and I do not know how to get out of the situation.
- Why do I believe that I am not good enough, or powerful or significant when my mind tells me these are not true?
- Why is it easier to forgive other people than it is to forgive myself?

Do you have any of the same questions? If so, you can go to the back of the book under resources and find my answers to these difficult questions. The problem with looking in the back of the book right now is that you will probably not understand the answers.

Please understand this, I do not live in the same world that you do. The world that I live in is rooted in reality. This reality is self-evident and is not subject to contradiction. The world that you live in is illusionary and needs the validation of many people in order for you to be certain, it is real.

What I want you to understand is that these statements are not the ravings of an egocentric conman, or the utterances of a profoundly spiritual guru. As you will discover as you read the book, the statement, "I don't live in the same world that you do" is quite literally true. The same can be said for the statements, "I live in reality" and "you are living in an illusion."

When you finish reading the book and read my answers to the difficult questions, the answers will be clear and reasonable.

A sensible question to ask at the beginning of any book is, "Who is the author?" and "By what authority does he speak?" Other reasonable questions are, "What is the book about?" and "How will it be helpful to me?"

Let me answer these questions by doing what I do best, telling stories. Since all stories have to have a beginning, allow me to start the story by telling you a little bit about my life,

I am having an incredible life. What has made it wonderful is all of the many and varied life experiences I have had. As a therapist, I have held juvenile delinquents in my arms as they cried out in pain because life did not make any sense. I have had the honor for the last 15 years of working almost exclusively with surviving victims of sexual abuse involving mostly incest. I have participated in their journeys from self-defeat and destruction to self-empowerment.

As a minister, I have watched people seek for certainty in their relationship with God and had the privilege of holding some of them as they died with a rare kind of peace. I have been present at the birth of children and felt the parents' joy and anticipation for the future. I have been honored to baptize children and felt the church's joy and hope for the future. I have also seen churches die and close, including my own, The Deerfield Methodist church when I was about 12. I have buried newborn babies including my friends' Lisa, and Terry's baby, Andrew. I have married many couples and then counseled some of them as they became divorced. I have experienced the weaving and felt the weight of the blanket that I am wrapped in, the beautiful blanket that is called life.

Amidst the complexity of life the one question I could never find an answer to is, "Why are most people unhappy?"

In my workshops I have often asked this question: "How many of you know someone who is fundamentally happy, not just happy for a moment, but experiences life with happiness?" Most of the time, one out of 25 people will maybe raise his hand.

That means that 24 people do not know anyone who is fundamentally happy. I then ask this question,

"How many of you were told by your parents or told your children that you wanted them to grow up and be happy?" Most if not all of the people in the workshop will answer in the affirmative.

I then tell them that having your parents give you this message of hope is like my giving you the keys to my car and asking you to back it out of the garage. There is a problem. You have never seen a car, do not know what a car looks like, or even know what the function of a car is.

What are the chances that you will be able to successfully find and start the car, let alone back it out of the garage without wrecking both car and garage? Somewhere between slim and none are the realistic odds. Yet, this is the mission we were given by our parents, and we, in turn, give to our children.

No wonder so many people are unhappy. They have been given a problem without a solution. For most people it is truly "mission impossible." I should know and in fact was expected to live the answer. It seemed fraudulent to me that, as a minister and therapist I did not know the answer.

I finally have found the answer for me and have found a process by which others can do the same. This is not snake oil medicine. The answer seems obvious now. The answer usually is, once you ask the appropriate question. The appropriate question regarding why people are unhappy is, "What are people addicted to?"

It was easier for me to discover and ask this question than for some because I am a recovering alcoholic and have been for 22 years. My addiction has helped frame how I view the world.

So what are people addicted to?
They are addicted to certainty.

Addicted to Certainty

Our lives have become so complex and confusing that the yearning to be certain is manifesting itself everywhere we look. It is in a government, which feels it knows how to create a safe and prosperous future. It is preachers both Christian and Islamic crying out for a return to old fashion fundamental truths. It is in the belief that science can solve all of our present and future problems given enough money and time. It is in the minds of adolescents watching as rock stars and self-made millionaires define what success and happiness look like.

An almost universal cry of desperation is, "I have to be right, because if I am wrong something terrible will happen to me." The amount of money spent on therapy and spiritual practices is beyond counting. The world, like your parents, is telling you that a secure and prosperous future will make you happy. This is the buzz the addict seeks - a future, state of being, that is better than the present. It does not matter to the addict that the future never lives up to its promise.

The definition of addiction is when you are unable to control your interaction with something. You are dependent on it. I believe that the world for thousands of years has been addicted to certainty. It does not want truth or reality; it wants to feel certain about something. Certainty is comfort, security, and a solid place to stand. People want to be able to say, "This I know." "This is who I am." or "Here I stand."

The problem with this is that the more you experience life, the more you discover that, whatever you know, or wherever you stand, life's experiences change you.

What you knew for certain when you were 16,"I will love Tammy forever" and what you know when you are 30 and Tammy is a distant memory, are different.

Is there anything that you can be certain of that will not change? Yes, there is.

The one thing that you can be certain of is your existence. Because you are aware you are thinking, you must exist. This may sound strange, but if you think about it as you read the book, you will discover that this simple statement lays down the foundation for discovering who you are.

It is also vital for you to discover that you perceive the world though a self-made screen. This screen has been created unconsciously by you most of your life. It effects and distorts every perception you have about the world and yourself. It is the source of your unhappiness and self-defeating patterns. It is what determines whether you are successful or stressful. I can help you recognize your screen and show you how you can change it. I can show you how to love yourself and other people easily. I can show you how to discover who you really are and always have been.

I am not interested in giving you hope; I am giving you a process and the tools to change your life. This process is not magic. The results of the process are developmental and continue for the rest of your life. Let me try to explain the concept by telling you a story about Esmirelda.

I live at Bear Creek Farm and a while ago, we had a cow we named Esmirelda. I received her as a gift from a dairy farmer friend of mine. He was troubled that we had dairy goats, instead of cows.

So one day when I was visiting him, he put this little calf in my Volkswagen Rabbit as a joke and a statement about real farmers having cows not goats. I took the calf home and we put her in the pasture with our goats and three horses.

Esmirelda grew up with the horses and believed that she was a horse. She hung out with them. She tried to run like them and in every way seemed happy as a horse. We thought this was funny and endearing. Then it came time for her to have a calf so we could get the wonderful milk that Bob was always teasing us about. He hated goats' milk. We took Esmirelda back to his farm and put her in with his herd. She was traumatized by all the strange animals. She hung out by herself or over by the fence where she could see Bob's two horses. When we put her in with a bull, she freaked out and refused the advances of this strange and aggressive animal. Eventually we had to take her home and raise her as a pet, because we could not convince her that she was a cow, not a horse.

Imagine what would have happened if we could have convinced her, that she was a cow by putting something like a magic mirror in front of her.

The function of the magic mirror would be to allow her to experience herself as a cow not as a horse. She then could have fulfilled herself as a cow by having a calf, being milked, and belonging to an appropriate herd.

Was Esmirelda happy as a cow who thought she was a horse? Probably, but the reality is that she was limited in what she could experience.

You were born as a happy person with the capacity to become fulfilled. Yet you have lived your life believing you are supposed to be whatever you are turning out to be. You are doing this because you sincerely believe you are "not good enough" or "you are damaged." You believe this to be true in part because the world seems to support and reinforce this truth.

However, because you have picked up this book, something inside of you knows you truly are a cow not a horse. You are more or at least different from what you believe yourself to be. I happen to agree with you.

I can show you how to look at yourself through the "Magic Mirror" that is your mind. Once you see who

you really are and have always been, you will be changed. I can then teach you how to build a new relationship with yourself and the world around you.

In order for me to do this, you will have to learn some new concepts and definitions. What I will teach you is simple, but not easy. What I mean is this; the process is simple once you understand the concepts. The development after you have done the process is simple because it just involves living. It will not be necessary to discipline yourself in a rigid fashion. There are no affirmations to repeat or exercises to practice. You will know what is real for you and overtime this is what you will become.

Understanding the concepts may be difficult for you, because people are usually uncomfortable with concepts with which they are unfamiliar. Concepts like reality, *cosmology**, and *cognitive dissonance*† may seem strange and abstract, but they are defined for you in the footnotes and in the glossary at the end of the book. The context, in which they are used, helps them to become familiar.

The book is laid out in three lessons followed by a section of resources that my clients and I have found helpful. I encourage you to use this as a reference book. Read it once. Then think about what you have read. When you are unclear about a concept or step, go back to the book and reread the appropriate sections again. I encourage you to use the glossary, the section on operational definitions, as well as the various descriptions of the journey.

---

* Cosmology is a theory or belief about the nature of the world.
† Cognitive dissonance is experienced as a feeling of discomfort when the mind is deliberately given antithetical or contradictory statements about reality.

You may discover it is easier and more effective to get a friend to read the book with you. This way you will have someone with whom you can discuss the concepts. This person can also be helpful in working through the process.

Some of you may want to try to master each lesson as you read. People have the freedom to explore and learn any way they choose. It has been my experience, since the book is not a simple "3 steps self help" manual, that it will be more effective for you to read the book in its entirety.

It is important for you to become familiar with the language and concepts. Again, the language and concepts are not difficult; it is just that they are interconnected and new.

Working with this process by mastering each lesson without understanding the overall goal, is like weaving a rug and not having a clear idea of what it will look like when you are finished. The product may be pretty and interesting, but will it function as part of the room in which it is going to be placed?

I encourage you not to be discouraged in reading the book and trying the process. You did not get discouraged when you were learning to walk. So carry that same level of anticipation into learning how to walk in reality and experience yourself differently.

In order to begin, it is necessary to know where you have come from, so what follows are descriptions of where we, as individuals and as a species have come from and where we are now. The main point I would like you to understand in the first lesson is that your awareness can grow and develop.

This developmental process begins at birth and continues as long as you allow it to. For most of us, the process stops or it has slowed to a crawl by the time we are thirty.

I will show you how to remove the limitations and to support the process of development later in the book.

For now, please read the first lesson and discover that you are on a developmental journey of awareness. It is not necessary to read all four examples, because each example was chosen for a specific audience. All of the descriptions are saying the same thing; they are just saying it differently. It is not mandatory to understand all of the four. Please feel free, however, to read all four if you are curious about how other people experience and express the journey of awareness. However, I would encourage all of you to read Everet's Story.

This recommendation is not given, as my wife suggests, so I can talk about my grandson, but rather because it is our story; each of us started life in a way similar to the way Everet has.

Lesson 1
Descriptions Of The Journey Thus Far

Everet's Story
(A story about Everet's birth and early childhood)

One day Everet woke up. He did not even know he had been asleep. He suddenly woke up and found himself in a strange and mysterious world. There was just himself and this world around him, made up of sounds, colors, and feelings.

After a while, he made a marvelous discovery. He was in, or maybe was or maybe had, a body. This was very exciting though confusing. How do you use it or what is it? Of course, Everet did not ask himself these questions, but the questions were there, nonetheless. He was amazed, "Who knew that toes were good for sucking, that fingers could touch things or that being hungry could hurt."

As time moved on, and time is important in this story, Everet became aware that his body and he lived in an even stranger world, a world of things out there, away from him. This is where living became really fun and confusing. Everet spent his time exploring, and over time he discovered that he could not only touch and taste things, he also could remember things. This felt good, like when he saw his mother's face he remembered that warm milk was on its way.

Remembering was helpful, because it enabled him to make sense out of all this new stuff. Nevertheless, after a long while, remembering was not enough. Things were getting familiar, but they were still very confusing.

29

For instance, he discovered to his astonishment that he could not do just anything, he wanted to. Everet was learning a powerful and painful lesson. He was not the center of the universe. The most familiar thing in his world, his mother, had told him "no." Everet did not understand what no meant until he felt the pain and then connected it with no. This connection/association would prove to be one of the most profound experiences in his young life. The association of "no" with pain was hard for him to accept and believe, but he had to believe it. What other choice was there? Experience taught him to accept this powerful association. The experience of the pain and the "no" were undeniably real and bonded together.

Everet had to accept that something outside of himself had power over him. It had power to cause him pain. For Everet this was neither good nor bad; it was just the way things were. His view of himself and the world, however, was changed forever. He now knew for certain that his "I want" could be blocked by the world's "no."

More time went by. Everet was becoming more aware that everything was bigger, faster and was happening to him. Everet was becoming a "big boy" and so, he wanted to make things happen. Making things happen is difficult when you are three feet tall. Big people could tell him what to do and what not to do. They could pick him up and move him where they wanted him to be, even if Everet did not want them to. Everet could walk and run but there were always limits on where and when. Everet could talk, but there were limits on where and when for that too.

The world outside of Everet's body was full of things he knew about. He knew daddy, mommy, and the two dogs. Everet knew his room and when he was hungry. He knew a lot about the things in his world, but he did not know "who he was in the world."

Everet was very confused. He knew the rules, such as do not throw supper on the floor, and do not leave the yard. He also knew a foundational pattern in life. That pattern was cause and effect. If he did this, then that would happen. If he pushed hard on the chair, it fell over and daddy got mad. If he smiled at daddy, he got picked up and was given a hug.

Moment by moment and day by day, Everet was growing up. Yet, Everet could not figure out how to stop the persistent confusion. He was Everet and there was the world outside of Everet. That world was full of things and rules but the separation between him and world was always there. Everet needed to discover "who he was in the world," if he was to overcome the strange and persistent separation.

One day, maybe it was Tuesday when he was three or Wednesday when he was five, Everet put all the pieces together. He had different pieces like himself and the outside world made up of his parents, dogs, house, bedroom, and rules. He had been collecting these pieces for a long time. But he was like a blind man trying to put a jigsaw puzzle together using only touch. Suddenly in an eye opening flash all the pieces that would not fit in a pattern suddenly did. Everett could not see the whole picture but he finally had the edge pieces and a sense about what the picture looked like.

Everet, in an unconscious process of gathering all the information he knew about himself and the world, came to a conclusion. This conclusion made sense to him and it explained everything. He was, therefore, certain it was true. Everet was absolutely certain that "he was not good enough." He did not have to ask someone if it was true, it was self-evident. This conclusion, that he was not good enough, really did explain how he related to the world. There was Everet and there was the world and its rules. The edge pieces to the jigsaw puzzle that would become Everet, now fit together. It would be many years before the entire picture would be filled in. But eventually whoever he believed himself to be and to some degree, how he looked was now firmly established. The picture that was Everett would be titled, "Everet is not good enough." For now, Everett knew how to put the pieces together and he happily went about the business of organizing his life.

He always had to pay attention to the rules and most of the time he got in trouble when he did not obey them. Everet knew that when he did something right, mommy was happy; when he did something wrong, mommy was not.

Everet had figured out a long time ago that he got in trouble for doing the things he wanted to. There are the ever present rules and Everet, who experiences pain when he does not obey the rules. His conclusion continued to make sense and feel true. It was self-evident and clear, Everett was not acceptable to the world; or in his words, "I am not good enough."

This conclusion felt wonderful to Everet. He now knew, how, "he belonged in the world." The experience of separation was no longer there. There was the all-powerful world and there was little Everet who was not good enough. Everet accepted this truth in the same way he accepted the relationship between no and pain. What alternative did he have? There was no one else in his mind but himself. This statement of identity was true, it felt certain, and it worked for him because the confusion was gone. Truly, this was a remarkable day for Everet. The great mystery of "Who is Everet" was solved.

Everet's mommy and daddy would never know this day was special. They would never know that on this day, their son became part of the human family.

If they could have known, they would have been horrified. They had been trying in every way to teach their son that they loved and accepted him.

The world needs rules if the I that is me is to live successfully in the we that is the world. Rules and traumas teach each of us that we, in some way, are not good enough, because it seems that we are always at fault.

The irony is that, his Grandfather, me, the writer of this book, knows that Everet's negative conclusional statement of identify will happen and there is nothing that I, like his parents, can do to stop it.

I know that my grandson will use his conclusional I-am statement to organize his perceptions of the world and his place in the world. He will use his I-am statement as a foundation on which he will build a network of beliefs that will support his perception.

This is neither good nor bad. It is necessary. It is how we all learn to live together in society. Rules and limits are necessary if anyone is to have some measure of freedom and protection. All I can do as his "Opa," is to wait for him to grow up and then, when he is ready, teach him how to get beyond his I-am statement and his network of beliefs. The greatest gift I can give my grandson and you, the reader, is a process by which he and you can discover who you really are and always have always been. In other words, the reality is that you exist and are acceptable. Everet knew and experienced this truth before he encountered the word "no." You and he can discover this self-evident truth by utilizing the process I teach in this book.

The process of raising a child and enabling him to achieve some measure of success and happiness inevitably leads to a negative I-am statement. Children raised without rules will be taught by the society at some point that there are rules that have to be obeyed.

These lessons learned later in life carry a great deal more pain and *consequences** than in childhood.

I do not believe that society is bad or evil. It just is what it is. Society is a network of rules and people trying to live together successfully.

I do not believe, that what I perceive the world to be is real any more than I believe that my old I-am statement is real.

The previous statement may sound strange to you, but this statement is a product of what I teach. Each of you has a negative I-am statement. It is the foundation on which you have created your life. Change your negative I-am statement to a positive statement of reality and you will inevitability be happier and more content. For now you can be skeptical about the truth of my assertion, but when you finished the book, you will know why I can make such a strong statement.

Everet is currently ten months old. It will be many years before he is able or willing to recognize that he views the world from a negative I-am statement. He has many developmental stages to go through on his journey of awareness.

My assumption, for you, the reader, is that you are ready to explore and possibly take the next step in the development of your awareness.

Thus, the next step of your journey begins.

---

* Consequences are intended and unintended outcomes from a specific decision or action taken.

The Poetic Description Of the Journey Thus Far

In the beginning *I* was.
But *I* did not know who *I* was.
There was only myself in the wilderness.

Then *I* recognize others like myself.
It seemed easier to be *I* when *I* was with the others.
So *I* and the others became *we*.

The *we* was comfortable but confusing.
The *we* needed an *I*, to be happy.
Slowly *we* all found our place in the greater *I*.

After a while the *I* that was *me*
became immersed in the *I* that was *we*.
It was a small price to pay for being comfortable and safe.

The *I* that was *we* tamed the wilderness.
It judged and controlled the *we*.
The *we* believed in the *I* that was *we*.

But the *I* that was *me* deep in the *we* was unsure.
The immersed *I* that was *me* became restless.

Who am *I* in the *we*?
Am *I* separate from the *we*?
Am *I* greater than that *we*?

Will *I* be alone if *I* am separate from the *we*?

How do *I* decide?
How can *I* be certain that *I* am right?
How can *I* know *I* am?

Thus, the next step of the journey begins.

E. Jack Lemon

The Philosophic Description Of the Journey Thus Far

There is an order to the *universe**. The universe is not random. There is some general level of predictability as when you drop a ball gravity is always there and pulls it toward the earth. This order and the *fact†* that something exists separate from me, i.e., my desk or wife, is what I call reality. This order, which exists, cannot be totally comprehended, predicted, or controlled by me.

My piece of the universe, however, can be understood and from that perspective, I can control myself and my interactions with the rest of the universe.

I cannot absolutely predict how the universe is going to react to my presence and my interactions with it. The more I become aware that I am real, that I exist, the more satisfactory my interactions with the universe and myself become. The reason for this is that most of what we think of as real: emotion, conclusions, our past, and future are personal perspectives and do not share the same objective existence as rocks and trees. The closer my perspective becomes rooted in what is real, the less conflict I will have. In other words, reality and I are working together rather than my imposing my definitional template on it.

The statement, "From my perspective," maybe the most profound acknowledgment that I can make, concerning my relationship and myself with the rest of the universe. After all, when all is said and done, all I

---

* Universe is defined as all that exists in any given moment.
† The classic definition of fact is something that is verifiable by sources other than you. Within the cultural cosmology fact can also be defined as something you believe with certainty. From the perspective of the spiritual cosmology, fact and reality are interchangeable.

have and ever have had is my perspective. The only point of view available to anyone is his own. I would take it one step further and say with Rene' Descartes that without my perspective, I have no way of knowing if I exist. In other words, "I perceive; therefore, I exist."

So what do I know?

I know that the universe and its order are real.

I know because I have a perspective, that I am real.

The question becomes how can I know that my perspective of reality is accurate?

The answer to this question is important if we are to live within the universe rather than trying to live separate from it and be in constant conflict with it.

From my limited perspective, human beings are the only aspect of the universe that is aware of its consciousness. In other words, we are aware that we are aware. The problem with this is that what we are aware of is influenced by others and ourselves. This happens, because although we are born with the capacity for awareness, we have to learn through trial and error how to use it effectively. This is a developmental journey of the self becoming aware of itself, in other words a journey of self-awareness. This journey is traveled not only by the individual, but also by the entire human species. One way of looking at our collective history as humans is that it has been a journey from the dim awakening of awareness to the effective use of that awareness.

I believe that the next step in our journey is to discover that we truly are real. We have and always have had an appropriate place in a greater reality.

Thus, the next step of the journey begins.

E. Jack Lemon

Psychotherapeutic Description
Of The Journey Thus Far

Role Of The Mind

The mind is a result of consciousness (the cause of consciousness is not relevant to this teaching because it is a whole discussion in itself.)

Consciousness is another word for awareness. When you were first born, you were simply aware that you were alive. The mind's task is to tell the you (the you that knows you are alive), what you are aware of.

The mind creates order out of the chaos, so that it is not overwhelmed by confusion.

It does this by ignoring much of the stimulus that is available to the brain and organizing the rest of it into a familiar pattern. You are reading this book; however, there is a huge amount of stimulus available to you as your eyes focus on the page. There are the sounds of the world around you, the taste in your mouth, and the weight of the book in your hands to name just a few. Your mind is aware of these additional stimuli and ignores or mutes their presence so that you can be aware of the words you are reading.

The evolution of the human mind may have started with, "What is the world outside of me? How do I eat of it, drink of it, and keep myself safe?"

The second step may have been, "Who are we?"

Experience taught the first humans that together they are more successful in getting and keeping food, water, and safety than going it alone.

By observation of history, it seems that the primary mechanism for the evolution of the mind was simply, "what works."

The result of this "we-awareness" evolution was the birth of culture.

Self-identity was submerged into the "we" or tribal identity. This loss of the self in the tribal identity was inevitable and necessary if the species as a whole, and the individual human in particular, were to survive.

This tribal identity was workable, but always the price the individual had to pay was submission to external power. The external power was not only a physically more powerful leader, but also was represented by the creation of rules that all tribal members were expected to obey.

What worked for the tribe then guided the mind's evolution. Morality was born out of the necessity for cooperation for the greater good. An example of this would be, "Thou shall not steal." If individual members stole from each other or from the tribe, in general, there would not be enough stored food for the long cold winter.

E. Jack Lemon
Cultural And Individual Aspects Of The Mind

The primitive tribal awareness grew over history to become a cultural awareness. This allowed people to relate successfully with diverse groups of people in a given geographical area. Cultural awareness is much more complex than tribal awareness.

Because of the need for survival, the cultural focus of the mind dominated awareness, and the individual or self-awareness aspect of the mind was muted.

As the cultural aspects of the mind grew through history so did the individual aspects of the mind. They did not grow at the same rate. The two different aspects of the mind would often be experienced as two different voices each clamoring for attention and superiority.

Cultural mind is the sum total of the mores, beliefs, and laws that enable a group to live together successfully.

Individual mind is the aspect of consciousness that questions, explores, creates, and ultimately seeks to become self-aware. We define self-awareness as becoming aware of self.

The conflict between the perspective of cultural-awareness and the self-awareness has been an underlying dynamic for the development of technology, as well as the arts. Conflict is not necessarily to be avoided. The energy that is created when innovation impacts the status quo provides the fuel for a Darwinian selection process. History has shown quite often that only the truly brilliant and effective ideas survive. The innovators are often ridiculed or despised by the culture, and only after time is it recognized how valuable their contribution or viewpoint was. Individuals throughout history have paid a great price for their innovations. Charles Darwin and his "Origin of the Species," Robert Fulton, the creator of the steamboat, as well as too many artists and sculptors to name, have paid for their visions, with their pain. In the art world, it is a well-known cliché to say you have to die in order for your work to be recognized. Jesus Christ is an example of one who had a perspective that was different from the culture and seemingly paid the ultimate price.

The culture wants to maintain the status quo. It likes predictability, stability, and order.

An individual may like the excitement of risk, the satisfaction of discovering something new, or the pleasure of creation.

The resulting tension between the cultural awareness and the self-awareness is often expressed in terms of morality. Examples of these moral terms are right/wrong, virtue/sin, and good/ bad. Many innovations are initially treated by the culture as a threat to the status quo, and if something is a threat to the comfort of a culture, then it must be bad or wrong.

A historical example of this is the culture's condemnations of Galileo's belief that the sun was the center of the universe rather than the earth. For generations in Europe the governments and the Catholic Church believed that the earth was the center of the universe.

This belief was logical and normal, because it grew out of the Holy Scriptures, which declared that man was made in God's image; therefore, man and the earth had to be the center of the universe.

When Galileo looked through his telescope and observed the motion of the planets, it was self-evident to him that the sun, not the earth, was the center of the solar system. This self-evident observation of the universe, which was available to anyone who looked through a telescope, threatened the foundations of power and authority of the church.

The church demanded that Galileo recant and admit he was mistaken. When Galileo refused, he was placed under house arrest for 22 years. What Galileo discovered, because of the individual aspect of his mind, was perceived by the culture as a threat. The greater culture condemned him and declared that he was a heretic.

The morality of a culture is expressed by the following statements: "The most moral choice is the greatest good for the greatest numbers," and "the most immoral action is to think only of yourself."

The Development Of A Cosmological Screen

The cultural point of view must have as its cosmological assumptions that reality is:

Knowable - can be comprehended

Predictable - if you have enough information about the past and present, you can successfully plan for the future.

Controllable - if you have sufficient knowledge and power, you can make anything you want happen.

This assumption that reality is knowable, predictable, and controllable is so basic and fundamental that it is embedded in all aspects of society. It is a framework out of which education, science, religion, and morality are taught, expressed, and ultimately evaluated. In fact, these assumptions are so pervasive that if you challenge them you are considered odd. Let us examine briefly, what science believes about these cosmological assumptions.

Knowable

Einstein's theory of relativity was developed in 1912 and deals with the macro or observable world, which is the opposite of quantum physics which deals with the tiny or micro world of the atomic nucleus. Before Einstein developed his theory of relativity, the whole world believed with Newton that the universe was constructed the way we perceive it. Newtonian physics states not only that the universe is the way we perceive it, but also that we can take it apart, examine it, and know all there is to know about it. We could in other words, examine the universe by believing we were separate from it.

Einstein demonstrated we cannot know anything without taking into account what its references are. We cannot separate ourselves from the universe and measure anything in any objective sense. Specifically you cannot measure the speed of an object without measuring it in relationship to something else. An example of this would be a car traveling at the speed of 60 miles an hour. This measurement of the speeding car is only real when measured against the earth, which seems to be standing still. However, we know that the earth is in fact spinning very fast. It only seems to be stationary from our perspective. How fast the car is moving in reality depends on what relationship you have with the car.

Predictable

Quantum physics, which was discovered around the turn-of-the-century, is a field of physics that deals with the nucleus of atoms. In this tiny realm of matter, there is no such thing as prediction in absolute terms. Quantum physics teaches us that predictability has to be measured in probabilities rather than certainties. Two of the beliefs of quantum physics are:

that you can know
where something is for certain, but not when

or

you can know
when something happened for certain, but not where.

Both of these statements cannot be simultaneously known.   In other words, prediction with *absolute** certainty is not possible.

Controllable

Chaos theory which has its roots in meteorology demonstrates that the order of a system is dependent on its level of complexity, the simpler the system the greater the perceived order. The more complex the system the less control one has. The society of the 21st century is so complex that no one can have enough knowledge and power to control any aspect of society. If you do not think this is true, examine the theories of education in America today and compare them with their application in schools. When you compare theory with application, it is clear that there are too many variables in a given school such as, economics, administration, and teacher skill, as well as the many variables in individual students', background, motivation and learning styles, to account for in any single theory.

---

* Absolute in this context means without exception.

All three of these scientific fields, Einstein's Theory of Relativity, Quantum Physics, and Chaos Theory have demonstrated that reality, which is defined as how things really are, is not knowable, predictable, or controllable in any absolute sense.

Society has largely ignored these scientific "findings" and still blindly assumes that the universe is exactly how we perceive it to be. Our society today does not condemn scientific "truth" as it did in Galileo's day; instead, we just ignore it.

The cultural aspect of our mind, which was created through the interactions of our mind with the culture, is experienced by us as a screen or a filter. This screen exists between us and the world around us. Simply stated, this screen or filter is <u>our interpretation of reality rather than reality itself.</u> This screen has the same cosmological assumptions as the culture that helped create it. As a result, it functions as an individual *cosmological screen** through which all experiences are edited and interpreted to conform to the culture's cosmological assumptions.

The individual mind, however, is not totally constrained by either the individual's screen or the culture's cosmological assumption. It is, in fact, motivated to question and to explore its assumptions.

---

* Cosmological screen is the interpretive filter through which we experience our lives. In the cultural cosmology, the cosmological screen is framed by our core issue and webbed by our core beliefs.

E. Jack Lemon

Two universal questions that humans ask themselves are, "Who am I?" and "Why am I here?" rather than "Who are we?" and "Why are we here?"

It is clear that science and technology as manifested in the fields of Chaos Theory, Relativity, and Quantum Mechanics, are challenging the assumption of a linear and absolute reality as taught and believed in the Newtonian view of the world. Linear and absolute are two aspects of deterministic reality where it is believed that cause and effect can be known with certainty. Another way of defining Determinism is that the past causes the future. In order to believe in determinism one must also believe that reality is knowable, predictable, and controllable in an absolute sense.

It may be that the lives of Jesus and Buddha were products of individual minds that explored and questioned this cultural assumption of a linear and absolute reality. They then discovered and reported a different experience of reality.

The question, "Who am I?" is a normal and natural question. The question and the need for an answer signals the readiness for the next stage of the self's developmental growth. The familiar images of the self and reality have become too limiting. The mind hears the *Cultural Cosmology's** definition of reality being challenged by science. It also hears that spiritual masters are challenging the same definition of reality. The mind experiences within itself confusion regarding what is real.

---

* Cultural cosmology is the sum total of the mores, beliefs, and laws that enabled a group to live together successfully.

46

What is a person to do with the resulting conflict of a *cultural-consciousness cosmology** and an *individual-consciousness cosmology* † both existing in his mind?

In other words, what is a person to do with these two voices or points of view clamoring for dominance? On the surface, they seem to be antithetical or extreme opposites.

Even if one develops the individual-consciousness cosmology as his primary cosmology, the fact remains that one still has to live in the culture whose view of reality is different.

I would suggest that the resolutions to this conflict are found in the transmutations or growth of an individual-consciousness cosmology into a *Spiritual Cosmology* ‡

The individual-consciousness cosmology has as its basis the belief that the individual perspective is equal to or better than the culture's.

The Spiritual Cosmology has as its basis the profound experience of knowing one thing with absolute certainty. That one thing is the knowledge that I exist. This knowledge is not dependent on anyone's validation or approval. From this single point of absolute certainty, I can now experience and interact with the greater reality in a new way.

---

* Cultural-consciousness cosmology is a societal perspective of the nature of the world.

† Individual-consciousness cosmology is a personal perspective of the nature of the world.

‡ Spiritual cosmology is a perspective that develops over time as a consequence of knowing for certain that you and the universe are real.

E. Jack Lemon

Both the cultural and individual aspects of the mind believe that we live in the world.

The Spiritual Cosmology believes that we live with the world. Another way of saying this is, "I am living through my life rather than living in my life."

This *transmutation**, which begins from a single point of certainty, reconstructs our perception of reality. Transmutation primarily uses the methodology of trial and error, so growth can be gradual rather than transformational.

Definition Of A Spiritual Cosmology

I have defined Cultural Cosmology as a point of view that is linear and deterministic. That is to say, it is a belief that reality is knowable, predictable, and controllable in an absolute sense.

I have described a cosmological point of view that is radically different from this. As stated, this point of view is rooted in science and the singular experience of knowing for certain that you exist.

My experience of this point of view and my rational interpretation of it have led me to this simple conclusion: When I know I am real, and out of that realness, I encounter a universe that is real, there will be interaction between the universe and myself.

I believe I have experienced such an interaction. The nature of that interaction has been dynamic rather than

---

* Transmutation is any change that occurs gradually and in an interconnected fashion.

one sided or passive. The experience of this relationship between myself, who I know is real, and the universe, that I also experience as real, has led me to define that relationship as spiritual.

I do not assume that I know the complete and true nature of the universe. I do acknowledge that it interacts with me in a dynamic fashion. The experience of this interaction coupled with my rational perspective has led me to define my cosmology as spiritual.

Again, let me reiterate all I am saying in defining my cosmology as spiritual is that I know I am real, I know the universe is real and the interaction is dynamic.

I do not believe that a Spiritual Cosmology and the Cultural Cosmology are antithetical.

Rather I believe that a Spiritual Cosmology grows out of a Cultural Cosmology as self-awareness develops.

Development Of A Spiritual Cosmology

Spiritual Cosmological assumptions
- Reality is much more complex than we can totally comprehend.

- The only aspect of reality that we can be certain of is that we know we exist, because we are aware that we are thinking. René Descartes declared this truth when he said, "I doubt; therefore, I exist."

- Because we are certain that we exist, we have a solid and unmovable place from which to draw conclusions about the nature of our reality and the nature of the greater reality around us.

49

The complexity of the greater reality cannot be totally comprehended because of the limitations of our mind and brain. We also cannot comprehend the greater reality, because we are a part of it, therefore, are influenced by it. It is impossible for us to stand outside of the greater reality and draw conclusions about its nature. A wise old doctor drove this truth home to me as a young man. I was trying to prove the existence of God and the good doctor was humoring me. Finally, he grew tired of the conversation and handed me a glass to hold on my lap. He then took a large pitcher of water and began to fill the glass. He kept pouring until the water overflowed and soaked my jeans. I jumped up and yelled at him. He just smiled at me and asked these questions, "Can the glass hold all of the water in the pitcher?" "Can the glass, which is smaller, comprehend the pitcher?" When I calmed down and thought about his questions, I told him no. He then told me to, "give up this fool's task, because I was a part of creation, therefore, could not comprehend the totality of the creator, let alone prove its existence separate from myself." He then told me that my time would probably be better spent chasing girls.

Any absolute order or the structure we perceive with our minds is created by the culture and is by its very nature linear. This linearity* is not replicated in nature, therefore, is a product of our cosmological screen.

If you doubt the truth of this statement, let me offer you a thought experiment.

---

* Linearity is a perspective of reality based on a belief in the direct relationship between cause and effect.

Linear refers to a straight line. Aristotle's description of a straight line is A =A. This is the foundation of what we call logic. A straight line meeting another straight line creates an angle. If you will stop for a moment and look around the room you are sitting in, you will notice that it is created using straight lines. In fact, most of the things in your room, whether they are books or tables, are designed with straight lines and angles.

Now that you are aware of how the physical space you live in is logical and linear, look outside to the world of nature. See if you can find one thing that occurs in nature that is linear. You will soon discover that almost nothing in nature is made of straight lines. Mother Nature, heavily influenced by gravity, designs by using curves. Only man uses logic and linear design as a foundation for his creation and interpretation of the world.

Linearity is based on a belief in the direct relationship between a specific cause and a specific effect. Linearity assumes that one can know the cause of something and the corresponding effect as separate entities that have a specific interconnected relationship.

This belief is so compelling that conclusions are often jumped to and action taken without critical examination. After all, the cause and effect is so obvious, that it must be true. Social, as well as personal history, demonstrates this assumption is often not true. Examples are she is dumb, because she is blonde; if you get a good education, you will get a good job; if you are from the south you must be racist, or you are a Native American you must be an alcoholic.

Another example of how persuasive our belief in the reality of cause and effect can be is people's reaction to this simple statement, "No one can make me think, feel, or do, anything I don't choose to think, feel, or do." Most people's reaction is a vigorous denial that the statement is true. Even though the statement is a foundational tenet of Rational Therapy, and the truth of it can be easily verified, people insist that while it is theoretically true it is nonetheless false. It may be that even you, the reader, have a difficult time believing the literal truth of the statement.

Let me use this statement as a practical demonstration of how the "common sense" of the Cultural Cosmology is often inaccurate.

All of us have made statements such as, "You made me angry!" or "She broke my heart." When we make these statements to ourselves, we honestly believe that someone has the power to make us feel something.

In order for this to be true, he would have to have the ability to take a long flexible probe, slide it by an eye into and the brain, and manipulate the limbic area. By physically manipulating the area of the brain that is responsible for emotional response, it is theoretically possible to say truthfully, "Someone made me feel something." I do not know about you, but I tend to shy away from people who walk around with long flexible probes.

The word "feel" in this context refers to an emotional response. It is possible for someone to touch you and you would "feel" his touch. It is also possible for someone to pick you up and move you physically; in this circumstance, he can "do" something against your will.

52

The context we are talking about refers to the ability of a person to respond both emotionally and cogitatively to stimulus.

I am responsible for my reactions to whatever stimulus is presented by the world outside of me.

All another person can do is provide stimulus for me to react to. It is my choice as to how I will react to that stimulus.

 Any recovering alcoholic knows to his bones, the truth, that no one can make him drink. It is always his choice. The truth of the statement that, "No one can make me think, feel, or do, anything I do not choose to think, feel, or do," gives him the power to be free of his addiction. This freedom can exist only as long as he takes *responsibility** for his choices.

This "common sense" of the Cultural Cosmology enables people to continue their self-defeating patterns, without experiencing guilt. They feel trapped and unless somebody does something to or for them, they will remain trapped.

I am not saying that cause and effect do not exist.

Reality is in fact a dynamic chaos where cause and effect exist, but not in any absolutely discernable or predictable fashion. The only exception to this, where cause and effect can be specifically identified, is in a laboratory experiment.

certain

too vague

---

* Responsibility is what one will be held accountable for. There is an assumed relationship between a person and what he feels accountable for.

53

There is order in reality that can be perceived, but not predicted except in probabilities. If you want to test this theory, set a specific time for a meeting. How can you accurately predict who will be on time and who will be late or early?

If you are honest with yourself and critically examine your world, you will discover that what you think is predictability is, in fact, a range of probabilities.

Time, which is one of the necessary components in accurate prediction, is always experienced contextually, therefore, is fluid. Our cosmological screen, however, make us believe that time is only sequential. The arrow of time, which only moves in one direction from the past through the present to the future, is a part of our reality. How we experience time is described in many different ways. We save time, lose time, waste time and use time. Time can move fast, slow, or stand still. We experience timeouts as well as time in. The simple question, "How long is a moment?" is one of the great mysteries. Clearly, although time can be measured sequentially as a clock, the experiential reality of time is much more than this.

The Nature Of A Spiritual Cosmology

Language and definitions, which are the building blocks of thinking and communication, undergo a profound shift in the context of a Spiritual Cosmology. An example of analogous shift would be how the definitions and experience of sexuality changes for boys and girls once they have passed puberty. Another example would be the expanding and redefining of the word family after a person is married. Experience provides the context for language and definitions.

54

If the foundation on which the interpretation of experience is based changes, then meanings and definitions of words changes as well. Examples of two foundations on which the interpretation of experience can be based:

Cultural Cosmology- Reality is knowable, predictable, or controllable.

Spiritual Cosmology- Reality is much more complex than we can totally comprehend.

To demonstrate the shift and the resulting difficulty of communication, consider this question: "If reality is not absolute, then where does one stand to observe it?"

good discussion points

This question is an example of the difficulty one encounters when he goes searching for deterministic answers from a spiritual cosmological context.

The question, "If reality is not absolute then where does one stand to observe it?" assumes that a defined place is necessary for observation.

What if a place is a point of view that exists as a part of an ongoing process of growth?

From a spiritual cosmological context, the definition of place undergoes a radical shift. This radical shift opens up new ways of thinking about the self and its relationship with the culture. An implication of this new thinking would be as follows:

If a place were a point of view that exists as a part of an ongoing process of growth, then the ability to judge something as absolutely right or wrong would be lost.

This loss of ability would occur naturally because of experience, rather than as a principle to which one has to adhere. Over time, emotions such as anger and guilt would lose their power to control and paralyze a person.

A natural consequence could also be the growth of compassion and forgiveness.

A possible unintended outcome of this loss of the ability to judge right or wrong would be that this would threaten the ability of the culture to have power over a person. Cultures, as well as institutions, both sacred and secular have historically used judgment and guilt as tools for control. A large number of people who live out of a Spiritual Cosmology would threaten the culture's established morality. Examples of this consequence are found in the lives of Jesus, Gandhi, and Martin Luther King.

If we no longer used right and wrong as a basis for decision making, what mechanism could we use?

It may be that the mechanism for decision making would move from right vs. wrong, to what do I believe is real and reasonable?

Questions that emerge out of a decision making based on reasonableness and what one knows is real could be

- What do I know is real about the situation?
- Is my decision consistent with my current understanding of what truth is?
- Does my choice help me to learn more about myself and/or my world?
- Is my choice reasonable, given the current situation?

- Do I have the discipline to act on my decision even though it may place me in conflict with my past or my culture?
- Can I accept the consequences of my decision without guilt or *blame**?
- *Do I create a win-wih* situation*

Discipline in this context means the ability to act in a consistent but not in a fixed or rigid fashion. This ability is developed out of experience rather than imposed by will or culture. <u>Discipline in this context is a process not a determined strategy.</u>

How Does Your Self Image Change Because Of Experiencing A Spiritual Cosmology?

Looking at the self from a perspective of growth or journey is profoundly different from looking at it from a perspective of a deterministic reality.

When one is making decisions based on what he believes is real, he also knows that this point of view will change through growth. Because of this, blame, guilt, and self-rejection will naturally diminish through experience. The sense of certainty that absolutes provide begins to crack and be undermined as a basis for knowing reality.

This sense of certainty is rooted in a collaborative interaction between the individual's cosmological screen and the Cultural Cosmology. Together they form a self reinforcing circle of interpretation. The interpretation that the individual has about himself is mirrored to him from the culture. His behavior conforms to cultural expectations and this in turn reinforces the culture's beliefs.

---

* Blame is to fix or establish responsibility for an action.

*win - frequency with 57 expanded awareness

The Spiritual Cosmology is formed out of the singular and personal experience of knowing that he exists. This profound experience does not need a culture or anyone else to validate it. The awareness of who he is, becomes so real and certain that the sense of certainty that arose from his interactions with his old cosmological screen and the culture diminishes and eventually fades.

too vague a statement

Without this old sense of certainty about who he is and how things must be, one is free to observe the actions of the self without fear of judgment or condemnation.

The lessening of the power of guilt, shame, and fear to frame how we see ourselves will lead to observations that are more constructive and promote self-growth.

Questions or statements that begin with "should," "have to," "must," or "ought to," begin to leave one's vocabulary, especially concerning self-talk.

Without the framework of absolutes, one is free to observe the self, his culture, and the natural world, drawing new conclusions about how things interact and interface.

The question, "Who am I?" now has many answers and we are free to select which answer is most appropriate for the context in which we find ourselves.

We are free to select because we first experienced the undeniable declaration, "I am."

Thus, the next step of the journey begins.

Addicted to Certainty

The descriptions I have written of the journey are not
new. Literature and songs throughout the ages have
used the journey of awareness as a theme. Myths and
legends, specifically the hero myths, are all descriptions
of the journey. Do not doubt the importance of the
journey of awareness. Just look in the self-help sections
of any bookstore. Directions for the journey are to be
found in myths and legends, self-help books, and in most
religious and spiritual books.

Much of human creativity is directed toward the
discovery, expression, and the manifesting of the true
self. It is as if we all want to find home, and we
intuitively know that our true, authentic, and
preconnected self is that home. The authentic
preconnected self is what we were when we were first
born. Home is that place of certainty that results from
knowing I exist.

My grandson, Everet, is currently ten months old,
and as I watch him, it is clear he is quite certain that he
exists and the rest of world is there to meet his needs.
For him there is no sense of morality, of right or wrong,
but there is a strong sense of belonging. Home is where
he is, at any given moment.

Can we find this sense of home? Can we know
that which we find, is the true authentic and preconnected self? In other words, "Can we be certain that
the self actually exists and we will recognize it?"

The answer to these questions is, "Yes, you can
find it, and when you find it, recognition will be internal,
indisputable, and self-evident."

The efficient aspect about what I teach is that it
utilizes the one human trait with which we are most
familiar and comfortable, our ability to doubt.

It also recognizes that our mind and brain use the
concept of certainty as a mechanism by which to
organize itself. The mind does not really care whether

what it believes is *objectively** true. It just insists that it be certain it is true. This distinction allows the mind to reconfigure its definition of reality as it journeys through life. This process of subtly reconfiguring reality using trial and error in order to know what is certain is like trying to walk upright through shifting sand. It leaves us with a deep yearning for something that is immovable and solid.

What if the mind could discover such a firm place on which to stand? It would provide for the mind what gravity does for the brain. One would know what is up, down, and where he is. From such a solid foundation, the mind would reconfigure what it knows to be real. Reality would not be experienced as socially subjective, but the experience of reality would be personal.

The mind could truly know what is real, and that definition of reality would govern how the mind interacts with itself and the world around it

There is such a firm place to stand and not only can it be found, but also the certainty of its reality is indisputably self-evident.

However, in order for you to discover that there is such a place, as well as to understand what I am teaching, we have to agree on a common vocabulary with agreed upon definitions.

To facilitate this process I have put a footnote at the bottom of the page, the first time a new concept or technical word is used. The word will be italicized to alert you to the footnote. The definition will be brief with a complete definition in the glossary at the end of the book.

One other note, you may discover that some of the text seems very dense and packed with concepts and

---

* Objectively means that something exists or is known independent of a personal or subjective interpretation.

information, where other sections are narrative and easier to read. There is a reason for this.

I am a classically trained thinker as well as an improvisational preacher. In others words, when I think, in the classical sense, I write one way and when I think as I am dialoguing, I write another.

You may notice that some of the sections like the forward, Everet's story, and especially the transition from one section to another may be easier to read than some of the explanation of concepts. I wrote the meat of the book from the classically trained thinker part of my brain and then went back and pretended I was talking to you about the upcoming text. One of the benefits of writing this way is that it increases the possibility that different kinds of readers and thinkers will have access to the material. I have also given you numerous illustrations and stories to provide context for the concepts.

Now before you are ready to learn how to take the next step on the journey of self-awareness, it may be helpful for you to become acquainted with two fundamental concepts that drive and organize our growth of awareness, both as individuals and as humanity as a whole. These two concepts are the content of lesson two.

In the second lesson, I would like to lift up two mechanisms that seem to be universal. Again, these two mechanisms are central to the organizing and growth of awareness. They are the mind's need for certainty and the mind's need to find "what works."

To facilitate my explanation of these two mechanisms I am going to introduce you to three clients of mine, Edward, Sara, and Elizabeth. These are not actual clients but rather constructs that I have created from real people I have worked with. I have done this

not only to protect my clients but also to protect myself. Many of my clients will recognize a word, phrase, or situation that is similar to their own. No one person, however, can be identified as representing my constructs.

So allow me to introduce you to Edward, Sara, and Elizabeth. They will journey through the book with you, giving you a reference and context to understand better, what it is I am teaching.

Edward

Edward is a 45 year old male, single, and the older? of two children. He has a good job, his own house, and two cats. He came to see me because of low level depression and general unhappiness. He felt he was getting older and there had to be more to life than what he was experiencing.

Sara

Sara is a 35 year female, married with two children. She is the youngest of four children. She and her husband have a house in a small town where her parents also live. Sara is active in her local church and schools. She works part-time so she can care for her children. She came to see me after she suddenly remembered several incest events in her early childhood.

Elizabeth

Elizabeth is a 60 year old female, married with six children. She is the only girl in her family and has two older brothers. Elizabeth has been married three times; her current husband of fifteen years is a college professor. Elizabeth has never had to work and has been busy most of her life doing volunteer work. She came to see me because of marriage problems and during a session mentioned that her father and uncle had sex with her when she was young and it still bothers her. She wondered if it was possible that this could be contributing to her problems with men and specifically with her husband.

You will learn more about Edward, Sara, and Elizabeth as you read the book. As you learn more about these constructs, it is my belief that you will also discover why it is that I am a therapist and a minister. In what other two professions can a person have the honor of encountering such interesting and remarkable people?

ego statement

Let us continue by exploring Lesson 2, "Mechanisms Central to the Organizing and Growth of Awareness."

Lesson 2

Mechanisms Central To The Organizing And Growth Of Awareness

Certainty

Certainty is a sense that is experienced by the mind through the body when we feel something is true. How this sense is experienced is highly individual. It may be experienced as something being clearer, more solid or just feels right. However it is experienced, the feeling of certainty is used as the primary organizing principle of the mind.

The reason the mind uses certainty in this way is because the mind hates confusion. A confused mind can place the body in danger, and it runs the risk of being wrong. A mind that perceives the world through a cosmological screen does not want to be wrong. In fact, in certain situations being wrong is more painful than actually placing the body in danger.

An example of this is, when a young girl submits to her father's sexual advances even though she does not want to, because it would be wrong for her to deny her father's wishes.

A mind that experiences the world through a cosmological screen seeks comfort and predictability. It is important to note that both comfort and predictability are individually defined and expressed. One person's comfort is another's insecurity.

Again, let us use the example of the young girl. She is more comfortable with her father's approval, than the confusion and pain that might result from her denying his wishes.

How is the sense of certainty created?

Within the context of a cosmological screen, certainty is created when an interpretation of an experience becomes associated with truth.

If the interpretation of an event is given often enough, it becomes familiar.

If the interpretation is familiar long enough, then you come to believe it.

If you believe the interpretation long enough, the interpretation becomes true.

If the interpretation is true long enough, it becomes a fact, and we, therefore, are certain of it.

The sense of certainty is the product of repetitious interpretations. Certainty is not in a position to judge the objective truth of the interpretations. Certainty just needs consistency to grow in strength.

Many of you have known people who believe that they are ugly and hate themselves because of this. Have you ever tried to change their opinions about themselves? No matter how hard you try, no matter what you say or do, the words have no impact. The irony is that you end up feeling inadequate because you cannot convince them that they are valuable. You are competing against years of repetitious self-conditioning. This conditioning far out-weights your well wishing attempts.

It is remarkable that no matter how strong certainty grows, it only takes one exception to weaken it.

You can walk with unconscious certainty across a floor in your house for years, but just one time let the

would prefer another 66 example

floor slightly give underfoot and you will never trust it in the same way again. Another example would be that you have driven down the road unconsciously certain that the person coming the other way will stay on the other side of the white lane marker. You do this even though the person coming at you is driving a 1,500-pound car at 60 miles an hour. Let the person cross the white line and nearly hit you and you will find it difficult to drive with absolute confidence again.

I am not saying that you will be paranoid about driving, but rather that you now know it is possible for you to be hit; therefore, at some level, you will be on guard.

Because we are social, we seek validation for the interpretations of our experience. It is through this social interaction that specific interpretations grow to become *core beliefs** and ultimately self-fulfilling prophecies.

In one of my cases, a 45 years old male, the youngest of five children, was told that his birth was an accident. He believed he was blamed for the lack of wealth, which affected the whole family. He was told from the very beginning that he was neither wanted nor desired. He heard this so often and had it reinforced by his siblings, that he became quite certain, that he was unlovable, and should not exist.

This kind of certainty often leads to suicide. In this specific case, he chose not to commit suicide, but rather to go into the ministry in search of a God who could convince him that he was lovable and had the right to exist.

After 20 years in the ministry, he had not found a God in whom he could experience love nor had he found

---

* Core beliefs are a loosely allied network of beliefs that emerge out of and support the core issue. They share a similar degree of certainty with the core issue.

a compelling reason to exist. Therefore, he just buried himself in taking care of everyone else. He was quite startled to discover that his high level of certainty about his own unlovability was the blockage that kept him from experiencing the love he sought.

The sense of certainty is used in all aspects of our lives. When we review the past through our memories, we are quite certain that our memories are accurate. We will hold to this belief even when our brothers and sisters or other participants tell us our memory is distorted.

This sense of certainty affects the very definitions that we have about words and concepts. In order for me to demonstrate this, I need to explain my understanding of definitions. The examination of peoples' definitions of words and concepts plays a significant role in therapy. If a person changes his definition of a concept then he changes his experience of that concept.

I divide definitions into two main categories. The first one is vocabulary/academic, and the second is what I call operational.

Vocabulary definitions are those one that can be found in a dictionary. These precise definitions are the tools, which are fundamentally necessary for clear communication.

An operational definition is one that grows out of an individual's experience. It is precisely because it is personal and contextual, that it has power over how we communicate with ourselves. An operational definition has greater power for us than an academic definition.

The reason for this is that people respond both consciously and unconsciously to their own familiar meanings of concepts, rather than the objective meanings given by academicians. Individuals are certain of their own definitions, because they are familiar and they make sense.

Addicted to Certainty

The process that we use for creating an operational definition of a concept is similar to the process that we use for creating a belief:

- We first make the association between a concept and its meaning or behavior.
- If this association seems to work for us, we use it again.
- As we reassess and find that the association continues to work, it becomes familiar and feels comfortable and natural.
- The longer we use the association, the more we believe it and feel confidence in it.
- The longer we have confidence in the association, the more we believe and experience it to be true.
- At some point in this process, the association between a concept and its meaning or behavior, moves from just being true to our experiencing it as fact.
- We are now feeling quite certain that our definition is real.

Having gone through this process, when we experience our definition, we believe it, regardless of what academicians or other people say. We hold to this belief, even if society offers a different point of view. This is how bigotry, racism, homophobia, and class definitions are created.

It is helpful to note that because the associational process occurs in the midst of living, the mind is only interested in whether the association works. It is not interested in whether the association is objectively true.

This sense of certainty plays a pivotal role in decision-making. Henry Ford was once quoted as saying, "If you believe you can or believe you can't, you are right." Being wrong for many people is embarrassing and painful. They are reluctant to make decisions when they are not certain they are right.

Thus, the sense of certainty becomes a mechanism for limiting and defining what is possible. It is awesome to contemplate how many people have been born in this world with an ability to make a significant difference in the quality of our lives and did not because they believed with certainty that they did not have the ability.

It may be that the sense of certainty plays its most important role in defining for us what is real. Theologians and psychotherapists understand that what people believe, with certainty, is real and this is all the reality there is for them. Reality is defined by what you believe with certainty.

There are significant problems with defining reality this way. Chief among them is that it denies the possibility of our participating in a greater reality. We are thus forced to wait for the greater reality to break in upon us in some miraculous or dramatic fashion. The consequences of such a breakthrough are seldom completely positive, because they reinforce the belief that we are helpless.

The sense of certainty plays such an important part in our lives as we live moment-to-moment, day-to-day. Without it, we would be overwhelmed with doubt and confusion, unable to make decisions or evaluate possibilities. Unfortunately, our sense of certainty keeps us trapped in a deterministic world, where the past usually equals the future.

I am going to use Edward, Sara, and Elizabeth to demonstrate how the sense of certainty is used to maintain self-defeating patterns.

Edward

In Edwards's case this sense of certainty denied him his own personal future. He believed with an amazing amount of confidence that he was destined to be just like his father, who was just like his father. It did not matter that this belief depressed and paralyzed him. The fact that he lacked the ability to change his life was all the reinforcement he needed to prove to himself that it was impossible to be different from his father. Edward had been to one other therapist before seeing me and was discouraged because he thought he had been "cured," but it did not last. He did not really believe that seeing me would do any good. I believe that Edward's motivation for entering therapy was not so much that he was desperate, as he was bored. An indication of this was his statement in the first session, "What do I have to lose?"

Sara

Sara used her sense of certainty in a vastly different way from Edward. She used it as a way of motivating herself. Sara believed that she was responsible for the important things in her life such as, family, job, church, the children's schools, and her physical body. She was not only responsible for all of these things, but she also had to be perfect in fulfilling these responsibilities. The amazing thing was that Sara did not report a particularly high level of stress. She honestly believed that the way she was living her life was the way that everyone lived his or hers. She was so certain of this, that she was offended when I suggested she was foolish in attempting to be perfect while living in an imperfect world. Sara was quite certain that her memories of her sexual abuse had nothing to do with how she was living her life.

E. Jack Lemon

Elizabeth

Elizabeth's sense of certainty was utilized to keep her safe. Her philosophy of life can be summed up in the phrases, "I know what is mine and I'll keep it" and "if you keep moving, they can't catch you." Elizabeth lived with these two beliefs most of her 60 years. To quote Elizabeth, "They have served me well, so why should I change?" This attitude would affect our relationship throughout our sessions. It was not until Elizabeth was faced with an ultimatum from her husband that she decided to quit moving and redefine what "mine" meant. For Elizabeth, her sense of certainty was so valuable, that she was almost willing to give up someone she deeply loved, to preserve it.

Although the sense of certainty is usually invisible, it is nonetheless one of the most important organizing principles of the mind.

The second organizing principle is really a tool that the mind uses to sort and evaluate consequences for specific actions. The mind needs this kind of mechanism to help it plan for the future and evaluate alternatives in the present. Like the sense of certainty, the mechanism of "what works" operates in the background of our mind and functions whether we are consciously aware of it or not.

What Works For Me

define

The mechanism of what *works for me* needs to be seen in reference to a specific process. The specific process, however, can be as minute as cell division and as all encompassing as a system of government such as democracy.

This mechanism of selection can be found in all aspects of our lives. It can be as mundane as choosing which clothes to wear or as vital as deciding whether to stay married to someone.

The concept of *works for me* has several implications: it implies reflection, evaluation, and some action based on the reflection and evaluation. *Works for me* can be a mechanism that promotes awareness and growth, which are the foundations of education. It can also support the status quo. Examples of this would be the old sayings like, "We've always done it this way" and "If it ain't broke don't fix it."

Works for me is the subtle criteria in any system that evolves. These systems are as diverse as a child learning to walk and the evolution of the species.

Works for me is a mechanism that contains no information as to whether what works is a good process or bad process; it just is a process.

Works for me always has to be seen within the context of its referent. Illustration of this would be the following:

Jennifer grew up in the shadow of an overachieving older sister. She believed she could not compete academically with her sister. Because of this belief, she made the decision to be prettier than her sister. Jennifer worked very diligently, paying attention to her hair, clothing, and weight.

She soon became aware that this was working for her. She liked the attention that she received and even had aspirations of being a model. However, she was quite unprepared for the male attention she received when she started dating at 14.

She responded aggressively to what she perceived as inappropriate attention from boys. She was soon labeled "the pretty bitch" at her high school. Quickly she became aware that behavior that used to work for her had now become a liability. She felt trapped because she perceived herself as pretty but dumb. Being pretty was now uncomfortable and was not working for her.

It is interesting to note that the evaluated aspect of what *works for me* may be triggered by a single event such as the embarrassment you experience when your wife confronts you for wearing stripes and plaids together, or it can be experienced over a long period of time such as learning to ride a bike.

The mechanisms, certainty, and *works for me* operate effectively whether we are conscious of them or not. However, once one becomes aware of his cosmological screen and actively seeks to transmute it into a Spiritual Cosmology these two mechanisms become powerful tools in that process.

Edward, Sara, and Elizabeth unconsciously used this mechanism to create their lives as self fulfilling prophecies.

Edward

Edward acquired from his childhood a belief that he was fated to be like his father, because his father was just like his father. He believed that he was helpless to resist this family pattern. When he explored other options while "bumming around," none of them felt right to him. Each option he looked at had too many unknown problems or risks. When he found a government job, everything seemed to fall into place. Life was simple and undemanding. Edward knew that he was on the right path because everything was working out the way he imagined it would. For Edward, the realization that he hated his job was irrelevant.

Sara

Sara believed her life was just fine, except for the annoying memories of her childhood. It did not bother her that she was busy 18 hours a day, seven days a week. When I ask her what would happen if she were suddenly to get sick, her response was, "That simply won't work, and I don't have time for it." Sara deeply believed because of her abuse that she was damaged and not good enough. Her response to this unconscious belief was to drive herself to prove it wrong. Up until now the strategy had worked. The resurfacing of her childhood memories, signaled a time of crisis. The mandate of her deeply held *core issue**, was about to reassert itself. What has worked for Sara thus far was about to change. The mechanism of "what works" would now change its referent. Her life would begin to fulfill the conclusion she was damage.

---

* Simply put our core issue is the conclusional statement of self-identity that each one of us makes to ourselves somewhere between the ages of two and five.

Elizabeth

Elizabeth very clearly and easily identified "what worked" for her. "If I keep moving they can't catch me," was her philosophy of life. This strategy actually did work quite well for Elizabeth. She did not spend a lot of time reflecting on the past. Her attention was directed mostly toward the future. The only thing that was slowing her down was her love for her husband. In him, she finally found something that was more important than her safety. Elizabeth was discovering that "what worked," for her before, may not work in the future.

omit (You have learned a little bit about me and why I think what I am teaching is important.) You have read the descriptions of the journey and hopefully you are curious about the next steps in the journey. You have been exposed to the two universal concepts. Now you are ready to learn the steps that will take you from a person who has a cosmological screen and lives in the world, to a person who knows who he is and is able to live with the world out of a Spiritual Cosmology.

It is time for the third lesson, Steps in the Journey of Self-Awareness.

Lesson 3

Steps In The Journey Of Self-Awareness

These steps in the journey of self-awareness can be understood as answering the questions presented in the last stanzas of the poem.

> Who am *I* in the *we*?
> Am *I* separate from the *we*?
> Am *I* greater than that *we*?

> Will *I* be alone if *I* am separate from the *we*?

> How do *I* decide?
> How can *I* be certain that *I* am right?
> How can *I* know *I* am?

It turns out that the next step is not all that difficult to take. You will discover that a cosmological screen controls your self-identity and your perspective of the world. If you remove that screen, what remains is you. This you, is the pre-connected *authentic self.**

Simply put, the cosmological screen uses your social context as its foundation for reality, while the authentic self uses the fact of its existence as its foundation for reality. The difference between the two foundations for reality is similar to the difference between a painting of a mountain and a mountain. The cosmological screen is an interpretation of reality, while the authentic self is undeniably real.

---

* The authentic self is the experience of the self as uniquely existing in the world.

The experience of the self truly existing is so quietly profound that issues of lovability, acceptance, and adequacy are not relevant. Having experienced yourself separate from everything else in the culture, you know with absolute certainty that you are loved, accepted, and adequate to the only person that matters, you.

From the perspective of the cosmological screen, the experience of the authentic self sounds like a rationale for being selfish. The implication for this is that what I teach is immoral and unchristian. I maintain, however, that the implications for being your authentic self leads to a more ethical and spiritual life.

One of the obvious implications of this experience is that because you can love and accept yourself, you are now in a position to love and accept others more easily.

One of the subtle implications of this experience is because you love yourself, you are now open to the experience of being loved by the Creator.

By discovering that the only thing that you <u>know for certain</u> is that you exist, the conditions have been created for you to discover that you are part of everything that is.

Let me explain what I mean by "you are part of everything that is" by defining two antithetical cosmological perspectives: Mitakuye oyas' in and Deterministic Reality.

The Lakota Indians call being a part of everything, Mitakuye oyas' in (all are my relatives); in other words, we are a part of the circle of life.

Deterministic Reality believes that you can stand outside the universe and examine it.

Mitakuye oyas'in and Deterministic Reality are examples of cosmologies that create vastly different interpretations of reality. Mitakuye oyas'in believes that you are a part of everything and therefore you cannot separate yourself from it. Objective observation is not possible when you are part of the circle of life. Deterministic Reality states that you are separate from the universe and can make judgments about it.

What I am teaching is that the cosmology of Mitakuye oyas'in (all are my relatives) replaces Deterministic Reality as self-awareness evolves. In other words, the next step in the evolution of awareness is moving from Deterministic Reality to a Spiritual Cosmology. This transition is as dramatic as the identity of a husband evolving into a father. Both of these transitions involve specific events. The birth of a child causes a husband to become a father. The experience of knowing you exist changes your perspective from Deterministic Reality to Mitakuye oyas'in.

It is one thing to hear the theme from the *Lion King*, declaring that, "we are all a part of the circle of life;" being able to experience it, is quite another.

The methodology I teach is designed to help your awareness evolve from a Deterministic Reality to a Spiritual Cosmology. The steps are straightforward.

1. Understand that there is a Cultural Cosmology and you have a cultural screen.
2. Identify your core issue and some of your main core beliefs.
3. Identify your *core truth**.
4. Journey to "that place" where you experience your core truth.
5. Begin the process of developing a Spiritual Cosmology.

---

* The core truth is an identity statement that emerges out of the experience of doubting everything that exists, except that you are aware you are thinking.

These five steps are the heart of what I teach and practice. It has been my experience that anyone experiencing the five steps will have his life changed over time.

As I have mentioned before, I am a storyteller. I tell stories throughout my clinical sessions and workshops. These stories illustrate and help make clear concepts that I teach. So I am going to continue to use Edward, Sara, and Elizabeth and their experiences throughout the five steps.

You will also notice that two out of the three examples are victims of sexual abuse. While this may make some of you uncomfortable, it is the main population out which these teachings arose. They are by no means the only clients that have gone though this experience. However, since I believe that sexual abuse, specifically incest, is the most destructive experience one can have (I have and am, willing to argue this point with other professionals) and since it works with my sexual abuse clients, I believe that it can work with anyone.

In step one, you will learn that what you think of as real is just your interpretation of reality. You mistake your perception for the true reality that is.

STEP 1

Understanding That There Is A Cultural Cosmology And You Have A Cosmological Screen

Cultural Cosmology

Another term that is used sometimes for the Cultural Cosmology is society. This term is so overused, however, that its precise meaning is vague. When I use Cultural Cosmology, therefore, I mean that it is the sum total of the mores, beliefs and laws that enable a group to live together successfully.

When one is born into a specific culture, he grows up believing what that culture believes. The cosmological assumption in the culture of the western world is that reality is knowable, predictable, and controllable. This assumption that reality is knowable, predictable, and controllable is so basic and fundamental that it is embedded in all aspects of society. It is the framework out of which education, science, religion, and morality are taught, expressed, and ultimately evaluated.

How one views himself in the world is influenced profoundly by the culture in which he is immersed. It is not however, a direct reflection of the culture because how he interprets the culture is dependent upon how he sees himself. His self-image and his corresponding beliefs intertwine with the Cultural Cos-mology, creating an interpretation of reality that is knowable, predictable, and controllable and in many ways profoundly unsatisfactory.

Edward

Edward grew up in Toledo, Ohio. His parents believed that if you worked hard you could get ahead in life. Edward's father worked in the Jeep plant and his mother stayed home and took care of the children. He grew up in a Catholic neighborhood, and went to Catholic schools all of his life. He rebelled against a strict upbringing and left college in his second year to "bum around" for a while.

He finally found a job within the local government and in his words, "settled down to become his dad." He hates it, but since he is the oldest, he feels there is nothing he can really do about it. Edward stated that, "I can't change; I was destined to be just like him and that is just the way life is."

He had a painful breakup with a long time girlfriend. The scars still linger after ten years. His conclusion is that, "You cannot trust women, because all they want to do is change you."

When I suggested to Edward that change could be a desirable thing, his responses were, "Maybe for some people, but not for those who were born under the don't change star." "Some people are lucky, and get to have fun and exciting lives, while the rest of us do the work" and "if you fight life, things could get worse."

Edward views the world as not so much against him as it is just something you have to deal with. He does believe that if you work hard, you can get ahead. He just is not sure what "getting ahead" means.

Sara

Sara grew up in what other people call the perfect family. In the small town where she still lives, her parents were well respected. Since her father's death five years ago, the family dynamics have begun to change with her brother and two sisters drifting apart. Her mother is "blossoming" without her husband's control and Sara is not sure she even knows who her mother is anymore. Sara believes that she should honor her mother and father but is confused about what honoring means. She is a "good wife" but admits that because of "problems" she and her husband have not made love much except to have the children. She tries to make it up to him by keeping in shape and taking care of him in other ways.

Sara views the world as a scary place and is glad they do not live in a big city like Detroit. Sara keeps a close eye on her children and feels responsible for their future. She is uncomfortable with the memories she has repressed. Sara tries very hard to be perfect, believing that if she is, her husband will not have a reason to leave her.

Sara was open to exploring her memories. She believed that they were probably true because they kept coming back at odd times. It was very difficult for Sara to blame her grandfather because he was such a wonderful person. She stated numerous times that, "Except for these weird memories, her grandfather and grandmother were just perfect" and "that she was lucky to have a family where parents and grandparents were close and supportive."

Sara deeply believed that it was her responsibility to carry on the family tradition of being a model of a good family.

Elizabeth

Elizabeth grew up in a moderate sized Midwestern city. Her father and uncle owned a family business that was successful. Her mother was described by Elizabeth as "dumpy and mousy." She has no respect for her mother and rarely sees her in the nursing home. Her belief is, "If you got it, flaunt it." She sees herself as pretty and likes male attention.

Elizabeth has isolated herself from the rest of her family and feels no guilt about it. Elizabeth believed family was something to escape. "They would try and hold you down, if you let them," was a dominant theme in our early conversations.

When we explored the concept of trust, I asked Elizabeth if she trusted anyone outside of herself. Her response was like that of a punch line to an old joke, "Sure, I trust others, a whole group of them: I, me, and myself."

She is well known and respected in the town where she has lived for 35 years. Her children have three different fathers, but she makes no distinction between them. "They are all my children and no one can take them away from me," is a statement she has made numerous times. She loves men but does not trust them, because "they all want the same thing, money, and sex." "Love is for the young and the foolish," and Elizabeth believes she is neither.

Elizabeth is upbeat about life but admits, "That just when things are going well, something always happens to knock you down." The statement, "The future is what you make it, as long as they let you," was often delivered with a laugh.

Edward, Sara, and Elizabeth all live in a society that has beliefs and rules that govern and influence how they see themselves. Can you identify some of the rules and beliefs that have profoundly shaped them? Can you identify some of them for yourself? Some areas to explore might be society's beliefs about:

> Definitions of family relationships
> Definitions of success
> Fate or luck
> Trust or love

The Cultural Cosmology can provide the backdrop for your life, but you are the designer and builder of it. What determines what your life looks like, is your responsibility. A simple way to understand why and how you turned out the way you did, is that you have had a cosmological screen wrapped around you. I invite you to read the following section on the cosmological screen and then revisit the previous section about Edward, Sara, and Elizabeth.

Cosmological screen

Our cosmological screen is our self-identity. It is who we believe ourselves to be. It determines our interpretation of the past and our projections into the future. It sets our limits and boundaries and develops our definition for concepts and relationships.

Our cosmological screen is the interpretive filter through which we experience our lives. The cosmological screen is framed by our core issue and is webbed by our core beliefs. In many ways, our cosmological screen mirrors the Cultural Cosmology. It believes that reality is knowable, predictable, and controllable.

It also believes that the memories of the past are accurate and its anxieties about the future are appropriate.

Our cosmological screen knows that cause-and-effect exists and that most of the time, failure is our fault. This is the reason we find it hard to blame others for things that go wrong. We may project to others and even to ourselves that the situation, other people, fate, bad luck, or even the gods are at fault. But for most of us in the quiet of our minds, we know that we are at fault. We know this because in some way we are damaged or not good enough.

Most people blame others

An extreme example of this was a client of mine who came to see me because she was feeling overwhelmed and unhappy. She was not depressed, but life for her was a chore. She was pretty, well educated, and was very successful in her job. There were no obvious reasons for her state of dissatisfaction. She was happy in her marriage and seemingly content with herself and her life. She generally seemed psychologically well adjusted, yet there was a sense of gray in life for her.

While exploring for her core issue, she made this statement in a very matter-of-fact way, "I'm responsible for everything, even those things that I do not agree to and I am held accountable for what does not work."

She did not believe this to be irrational and quietly defended this statement with a firmness that was remarkable. This statement of a core belief would not be changed until she experienced her core truth while being in "that place." Subsequently she has reported experiencing life as lighter and easier. She generally laughs and smiles when she is reminded of her old core belief.

has this been explained? This lady's cosmological screen denied her any possibility of joy and happiness, no matter how successful she became. She could work hard and be dependable, but she was not allowed any pleasure in it.

One of the things I continually teach my clients is not to underestimate the power and pervasiveness of their cosmological screen. After you have experienced your core truth, a lifetime of habitual patterns can and will pull you back into an emotional bog. When you have a core truth rooted in a Spiritual Cosmology, you can pull yourself back from the emotional bog.

Using Edward, Sara, and Elizabeth, can you identify what is the Cultural Cosmology and what is each of their cosmological screens? Good indicators that one is viewing reality through a cosmological screen are when one feels emotions such as guilt, anger, or fear. These are usually felt when we are reacting to something. Often what we are reacting to are the rules or expectation of the Cultural Cosmology.

Take a moment; try to get a sense of the difference.

So, you are in a Cultural Cosmology out of which you have developed a cosmological screen that is controlling your life. Your cosmological screen is made up of a core issue out of which is developed a full set of core beliefs. What are core issues and core beliefs? This is the topic of the next step.

I do encourage you to go back and reread the section on Edward, Sara, and Elizabeth before you move to the next step. In some ways, learning this process is like learning mathematics or a foreign language. It is important to understand each step before you move on to the next.

STEP 2

Identifying Core Issue And Core Beliefs

Pediatric neurologists and psychologists call preschool children "little scientists." The reason they call them this is because they are constantly running scientific experiments. These scientific experiments usually take the form of if-then situations. Examples of this would be if I cry, then someone does something for me, or if I throw my glass of juice, then mother gets angry with me. A small child uses these if-then experiences as a basis for ordering his life. After a number of years of data gathering, the little scientist draws a conclusion based on his interpretation of the accumulated data of experience. This conclusion is formulated, as an I-am statement, which is a statement of self-identity.

Prior to this conclusional moment, when the child was very young, he had a singular experience that would change his life forever. That experience was when he heard or felt the concept of "no" for the very first time.

Before this life-changing experience, the child did not know that he was not the center of the universe. When he experienced the word "no" from a power outside and greater than himself, he knew for the first time that something was wrong and it was probably his fault. This sense of being wrong provided the very first foundational data that would grow into the full-blown conclusional I-am statement later on.

This conclusional statement usually takes the form of a statement about the child's unworthiness of being an object of love.

The child tells himself this I-am statement with a very specific cadence, using specific self-descriptive words and a specific emphasis on the syllables. Some people have described this I-am statement as a mantra or spell that the child uses on himself so that he knows who he is.

I would suggest another interpretation; this I-am statement provides the framework for what will become his cosmological screen. He will use this framework to interpret his perception about the world and its interaction with him.

His interpretation, because of the filtering of the cosmological screen, usually will be that he is in some way unworthy of being loved or valued. He does not know why. He just knows it is true.

After years of interpreting the interactions of the world with himself in this biased fashion, he slowly develops core beliefs. These core beliefs are framed as if-then statements.

Examples would be if I try then I will always fail, or if I have friends, then they will reject me. These core beliefs grow into interconnected patterns that support the core issue.

The more experiences the person accumulates that are interpreted out of the context of the core beliefs and issue, the more his core beliefs and issue are reinforced. This endless loop of self-created experiences, interpretations, and conclusions continues until this very day.

This is how human beings
become self-fulfilling prophecies.

The process of creating a belief is well known and powerful. This same process is utilized in creating a core belief. It follows a very predictable pattern:

If you tell yourself something long enough, it becomes familiar.

If you tell yourself something familiar long enough, you believe it.

If you believe something long enough, it becomes true.

If you know something is true long enough, it becomes fact.

If something is fact long enough, and it is a pattern, then it can become a core belief.

This core belief becomes fact, immutable, unchangeable, and is the webbing of the cosmological screen, which is framed by the core issue.

Every interpretation of what you perceive, throughout your life is filtered through this cosmological screen. It determines what is possible, what is necessary, what is desirable, what is true, and ultimately your current self-identity.

It is extremely important to understand and remember that,

a lie has power,
as long as you are unaware,
that it is a lie.

There is no way to know that as a small child, using narcissistic conclusions based on limited perspectives, you would frame this screen. You had no way of knowing that this young innocent you, would lay down the framework that would become inevitably, you, today.

Simply being aware of the above can begin the process of healing. You have, however, a lifetime of habits and interconnected beliefs that will make it difficult for you to sustain this level of awareness.

Remember, you are dealing with self-identity; the mind will not easily give up the lie because it feels true. This I-am statement is foundational and you have a lifetime of conformational experiences to support it.

The only thing that can modify or replace this core issue is awareness or an experience that feels more true or real than the lie.

This awareness would have to be grounded in a personal experience that is rational. In other words, this awareness of reality must be so true that it cannot be questioned or contradicted. This awareness of reality would have to be self-evident and absolute.

There is such awareness.

It is grounded in the fact that the only thing I can be certain of is, I am aware that I am aware. Stated another way, I am aware that I am thinking and perceiving.

Rene' Descartes stated this truism, in this fashion "I am thinking; therefore, I exist" or as it traditionally is stated, "I think; therefore, I am." The experiencing of this truism can be life changing.

One of the most profound implications of experiencing this revelation is that you know you are the only thing for certain that exists for in your world. You are a class of one. There is no one or no thing to which you can be compared. → explain this sentence

**Any core issue
that is based on a comparison
is by definition a lie.**

91

Conclusions drawn from this experience are *[handwritten: ?]*

- Only you exist in your world. *[handwritten: question]*
- The only real data you have about you and the world is your perception.
- The only thing you know about you and the world is your interpretation of your perspective.

The perspective from this absolute reality allows you to alter your cosmological screen. You can use this new perspective to view the patterns of your life. You can also learn to live in the present moment and thereby create a new future.

Now you know what a core issue and core beliefs are and that they can be changed. The next question is, how do you identify your core issue and your core beliefs?

I believe that a sufficiently motivated and self-aware person can discover his core issue, core truth, and go to that place on his own. It is, however, a lot easier, more efficient, and more fun, when it is done with another person. The other person does not have to be trained to do this, but he does need to be knowledgeable about the concepts and techniques. Participating in this process with somebody who is trained and has gone through the process himself or herself, however, can be more efficient.

Much of human behavior is governed by habitual patterns. These patterns are recognized not only through behavior, but also through language. Language is a product of thought; so, listening to someone over a long period or having him share the habitual statements that he makes to himself, give us clues as to his core beliefs. Most of us know our core beliefs, either because we continually say them to ourselves or because we keep manifesting them and it frustrates us. In a short time, conversations that involve some reflection can enable one to create a list of three or four core beliefs.

Once you have a list of three or four core beliefs, you can begin to examine them and find what simple statement is at the root of the core beliefs. This simple statement is usually phrased in an I-am format. When you try out examples of core issues by saying them aloud, you will usually respond by saying, "No that's not it" or "It's close but it is not quite right."

This process of exploration continues until you feel or state with a strong sense of certainty that the statement of your core issue is true. Usually you will give a body language clue when the correct statement is expressed.

I would reiterate that this process is most effective when it is done with someone else because the body language clues may be difficult to observe in you.

These clues may run the gamut of a nervous laugh with eyes turned to the floor to an up thrust chin with a voice of defiance. One of my clients after stating to me that he did not believe he had a core issue, suddenly stood up and screamed at me that what I suggested might be his core issue, "was not true" and "could not be true." After he was through screaming, he sat down and broke into tears. It was clear from his body language, we had found his core issue.

If there is not the physiological response to the expressing of the core issue, I do not believe that it has been identified. It is quite common for a person to believe sincerely that he has found his core issue when in fact he has identified a significant core belief. It has been my experience with all of my clients that their body reacts when their most hidden and treasured secret is exposed and expressed.

I encourage you to sit with you core issue for about a week. Think about it, exam it, and see if you get the same physical/psychological response. You will know if your core issue is correct, because it does not change and it feels "right."

Suggested steps to discover your core beliefs:

1. Examine the main patterns of your life, specifically patterns that are unfulfilling or annoying. Especially note patterns that you have been unable to change.

2. Check with family or friends to see if they are aware of these patterns.

3. Solicit patterns that they have noticed and you are unaware of them.

4. Make a list of three or four that feel, look, or sound the most powerful and true.

5. Discern what I-am statement is foundational to these beliefs; foundational means that all of the beliefs are raised out of this simple I-am statement.

6. Be aware of any physical response when you state your core issue.

7. Live with the core issue for about a week and see if it still feels true.

Edward, Sara, and Elizabeth went through this process with me. It is a good exercise to look at their core beliefs and then review their stories. Discern whether you can see their core beliefs embedded in the narration. Use the same process to see if you can see the connection between their core beliefs and their core issues.

Edward

Edward was able to identify a number of core beliefs some of which he knew were from his early childhood; others were developed later in life.

Edward's Core Beliefs

- I am helpless to affect long-term change in my life.
- A kind of genetic destiny controls me.
- Because I fight this destiny, I will always be alone.
- I cannot be happy, because no one in my family has ever been happy.

We began to explore what simple I-am statement could account for all of these core beliefs. Core beliefs have made it impossible for Edward to know who he is separate from his family. When he uttered for the first time his core issue, his shoulders slumped and he quietly said I know it is true.

Edward's core issue is "I am helpless."

Sara

Sara was able with my help to uncover her main core beliefs. They were subtle because of the repressed memories of sexual abuse.

Sara's Core Beliefs

- I have to be right or something terrible will happen.
- It is my fault my grandfather molested me.
- I am responsible for the important things.
- If I am perfect, then things will not change.

There clearly seemed to be a great deal of judgment and a strange belief in a magical cause and effect that indicates Sara's abuse occurred at an early age. It was later determined this was accurate. Sara believes it started happening when she was about three years old. Once this was established, her core issue was easy for her to see. When she said it for the first time, there was a note of relief in her voice and body, as if a long held secret was now revealed; therefore, she did not need to hide from it anymore.

Sara's core issue is, "I am damaged."

Elizabeth

Elizabeth's core beliefs were difficult for her to sort out. The reason for this was although she knew she had been sexually abused, her generation did not acknowledge its existence. Thus, she treated it as if it were just something that happened and if she ignored it, then it would just go away. In her words, "If you do not think about it, it must not be a big thing." Unfortunately, for Elizabeth this belief was not true. After sharing with her the deep destructive consequences of sexual abuse, she was able to make sense out of the patterns of her life.

Elizabeth's Core Beliefs

- I cannot trust anyone especially my family.
- You have to take care of yourself first, regardless of how it affects others.
- You cannot win because something will stop you.
- Love does not exist.

The surprise to Elizabeth was the cynical flavor of her core beliefs. Most of her life she had lived by the statement, "Don't think about it; just keep moving." She

96

later told me that it is no wonder she had this philosophy of life because if she had thought about her life, she probably would have gotten so depressed she would have shot herself.

It took a week before Elizabeth finally felt the truth of her core issue. She tried to deny it, but as she thought about it and experienced saying it to herself, "It sank in and felt not only real but true."

Elizabeth's core issue is, "I am completely unlovable."

Now that you have your core issue and core beliefs identified or at least understand what they are, do you want to keep living your life with a screen that is a lie? Edward, Sara, and Elizabeth chose not to. I am going to assume your answer, like theirs, is no.

You cannot take away something as significant as a core issue without replacing it with something else. This is like taking the foundation of a house away and believing that the house will hang in space without falling. It will fall and the walls and roof will collapse. In fact, I invite you to try to remove your core issue and see what happens.

You will discover, as I did as a therapist that you might believe that you have removed the old pattern, but it will emerge in the very near future. This pattern will begin to reassert itself as soon as you no longer focus on it. It has to because your identity is based on a core issue that your mind is certain is true. The only thing that can replace this old pattern is some other I-am statement that the mind now accepts as truth.

This cannot be an affirmation or something you have learned in your enculturation process. The reason for this is that any powerful affirmation you were given or discovered for yourself may feel true, but it does not carry the same level of certainty that your core issue does, because it has been filtered through your cosmological screen. Any replacement for your core issue must be self-evident and noncontradictable by anyone, including you. A core truth is the only truth of which your mind can be certain.

What I am about to say, may sound mystical and vague but I assure you it is not meant to be. Your core truth is what you knew yourself to be in that predomesticated time. This was a time before you became socialized; this was when you were the true, authentic, and preconnected self. You may not have had language for it, but you knew who you were because there was no one with whom to compare yourself. You were a set of one. There was you and everything else in the world. Everything else in the world, however, was rather undefined and unstructured.

I know you can find your core truth, because my friends, clients, and I have found ours. The discovery of your core truth is like a big sigh; finally, we had returned home and rediscovered something that was clear and felt true. Each of our core truth statements was different yet even in the beginning before we had experienced it, each of us knew, ours sounded beautiful; it looked clear and sharp and felt solid. We each wanted to believe it.

Then I found a way for each of us, not just to believe it, but to experience and to know our core truths. It changes our lives.

If this sounds good to you, then read on and discover what your core truth is.

This one truth will, when experienced, set you free.
not right away but eventually.

STEP 3

Identifying Your Core Truth

The core truth is not the opposite of the core issue. It is what replaces it. The core issue is negative in nature. It describes the relationship of the self within the rest of the world. From the self's point of view, the world is more correct, more powerful, more real, or more something, and the self is somehow damaged, not good enough or should not exist. This is not something that a person continually walks around thinking, but it is the foundation for how and what he thinks.

The core truth is an I-am statement that involves only the self. It is an identity statement that needs only itself as a referent. *It is felt.*

This statement is self-evident and simple. There is also a body response when it is stated. It is often described as being crystal clear; it sounds right, or feels solid.

This process of identifying our core truth is most efficiently done out of the conversation with another person, but it can be accomplished by a person writing down examples of his spiritual truth.

Identifying your core truth has been compared to picking out your special stone from a basket full of ordinary stones. I have often used this process in my work with people.

The exercise involves giving the client a basket of assorted stones. He is then instructed to find the specific stone that is his. Everyone has a different style for choosing the stone, but eventually with encouragement, he chooses one.

I then challenge him to explain why he chose that stone. The conversation continues until he knows with certainty that that stone is his. If he begins to doubt his choice, he puts it back in the basket and continues looking.

Once he gets past choosing the stone based on what it looks like, or what he thinks will please me, he begins to use some other process. It may be intuitive or energy or something of which I am not even aware. The result of his using his own non-rational process is his choosing a stone that he just knows is his. It does not matter to him if I think, it is the correct stone, if it is pretty, or even if he has chosen the "right" stone. He just knows it is his stone.

The stone exercise is an example of what happens when an individual uses a process that emerges out of him. This process does not need to be labeled by me, but it does have to be experienced by the individual to know a process even exists.

For some people, the basket of stones has to be metaphorically filled by me, using examples of other people's spiritual truths. Sometimes a person can fill a bushel basket with his ideas. The number of examples does not matter. What matters is, the finding of his specific spiritual truth.

When he discovers what he believes to be his spiritual truth, there is usually a physiological response. This response can vary from a quiet smile to a shout of exultation.

I have learned from experience to encourage the person to sit with the spiritual truth for a week or so. Many times a person will come back to the next session saying that the core truth was close, but the language was not quite right. We then explore together until we find the precise language that works for him.

Precise language is as critical in the spiritual truth as it is in naming the core issue. I often tell my clients that this process needs to be as precise as brain surgery.

Close is not good enough, because we are not playing horseshoes.

Identifying one's core truth for most people is a pleasurable experience of exploration. A person comes to realize that he always has had a non-rational, but effective process for choosing. This experience alone is empowering. What is even more empowering though is the discovery of a self-identity that feels true. It is one thing to feel that something is true; it is quite another to experience the certainty of it. An example of what this process could look like is as follows:

1. Find some quiet time when you can be by yourself or with another person you feel comfortable with.
2. Say to yourself or write down your core issue.
3. Imagine what you would be like if you did not have your core issue.
4. Who would you be? What identity statements could you make that would be true?
5. Start the statements with I am…
6. Make a list of these I am statements.
7. Notice how you feel, particularly in your body as you say aloud, each statement.
8. Make another list of the one or two statements that feel the most real.
9. Try restating these statements in a different way. Specific language, speed of delivery and voice inflection can be very important.
10. When you have found the one that feels the most real, practice saying it and again noting how your body responds each time you say it.
11. Sit with this candidate for your core truth for about a week. If there is still some doubt, play with it some more until you are certain you know what it is. Say it to yourself or write down your core truth.

For some of my people finding their core truth is easy and for others it is difficult. Let me illustrate this point by continuing Edward, Sara, and Elizabeth's stories.

Edward

Edward had a great deal of difficulty finding his core truth, partly because he truly believed he was helpless. It was very frustrating for him because I refused to supply him with other people's core truths. I insisted that he find his own way to know which stone was his stone. After a number of difficult sessions, Edward blurted out in disgust that,"I guess I will just have to be me." I noticed his head jerk as if he had been slapped lightly on the side of his head. I asked him to repeat what he had just said. He looked at me for a moment and then said with a smile, "I am me." In that moment, we both knew he had found his core truth. I had him wait a week and at the next session, I asked him what his core truth is. He just looked at me and quietly stated, "I am me and that is just fine."

Edward's core truth is, "I am me."

Sara

Once Sara understood what a core truth was, it was easy for her to declare hers. The key for Sara was for me to ask her this simple question,"If you take away your core beliefs and your core issue what will you be?" Her answer after a moment or so was, "I would be worthy of love." I asked her to explain and when she was finished, I asked her simply to summarize what she had just shared with me. She looked me right in the eye and clearly stated, "I am loveable." She then giggled and suddenly stood up and said, as if she wanted everyone to hear, "I am loveable."

Sara's core truth is, "I am loveable."

Elizabeth

Elizabeth and I had difficulty discovering her core truth. The reason for this is that her core issue struck at her very existence. If you truly believe that you are completely unlovable, then what reason is there for you to exist? She may have been right when she stated, "If she had thought about her life, she probably would have gotten so depressed she would have shot herself." Once we had explored the implications of being completely unlovable, I asked her what was left. What could she say to herself that was true and real? She could not think of an answer. I did not see her for two weeks and then at our next session she started with, "I got an answer but it does not make any sense." The answer came to her while she was lying in bed the night before. The answer was, "I am." When I asked how it felt she said, "Solid as a rock." I then asked, "Why it did not make sense?" Her reply was that, "It was too simple." We then talked about the profoundness of her core truth.

Elizabeth's core truth is, "I am."

We have identified the core issue and the core truth. Now it is time to drain away the certainty of the core issue and replace it with the experience of the absolute certainty of the core truth. This is a process, which enables you to experience a <u>place</u> where you know for certain you exist.

I call it "that place" because I do not know what else to call it. It is a place because you are there, but it is not located in space or time or strictly speaking in your mind.

I have no way of knowing if "that place" is the same for everyone. I only know it exists because I have experienced it. People have tried to describe to me what they are aware of when they are in "that place" and they report, that only they are there. They may be aware of light or dark, but the only thing that they are truly aware of is the quiet reality that they exist.

Some of the ways that I know that a person has arrived at "that place" is that his body becomes very relaxed and his voice becomes quiet, clear, and confident. When I asked him if his core issue is possible, his response is generally a quiet no or simply a shake of the head. When I asked him to state his core truth, the response is immediate and affirmative. There is not a lot of emotion expressed, but he is able to convey a profound sense of certainty in voice inflection and body language.

All of the steps you have learned so far can have a powerful impact on your life. Just knowing you have a cosmological screen and knowing what your core issue is, brings a new perspective to how you interact with the world. Discovering your core truth can create a gentle kind of cognitive dissonance that manifests itself as a deep yearning to be, what you know you are. All of this is true, but without experiencing the absolute certainty of the core truth, all you will have is the yearning. This discomfort of the unfulfilled yearning will create doubt over time about the certainty of your core truth. Your core issue will inevitably reassert itself. If this happens, the process I am teaching you will just be another self-help technique that failed to live up to its hype.

104

Going to "that place" is not a meditation technique
if you are defining meditation as closing your eyes and
trying to silence your mind.

In fact, to discourage you from experiencing this as meditation, I encourage you to do all the steps except the sensory deprivation tank with your eyes open.

Going to "that place" is not an out of body experience; rather it uses body awareness as an important aspect of the process. You will be instructed to move from one area of awareness to another when you are physically and emotionally uncomfortable.

The journey of going to "that place" is a process that asks you to focus or put you attention in a specific area that you usually only flow through.

In order to illustrate this, I would like you to read the following section using your mind, your memories, and your body to help you fully associates with the story.

You may be aware of your body when you are driving your car. This awareness usually lasts only as long as it takes to get comfortable. Your attention then focuses on the world outside your body as you back out of the garage and drive down the road. Very quickly your attention flows into thoughts about your day ahead as you plan your "to do" list. You notice that you are a little sluggish this morning and decide you need a strong cup of coffee to wake up so you put your attention to finding a gas station or coffee shop. While in the coffee shop, you are aware of the smell of donuts so you argue with yourself about the "need" for something sweet. While this debate is going on, you hear an old song playing over the noise of people's conversation. This old song brings back a memory of a love you once had. While you are making change for the coffee and donuts, your mind is reliving the pain of your broken heart. You carry this sense of melancholy into the car and it lasts until someone cuts you off and almost forces you off the road. Fear and rage immediately replace sadness.

And so it goes, moment by moment, day after day the seemingly seamless flow of your attention. All of these moments of attention feel real and this creates the assumption that everything you are experiencing is equally real. But of course, it is not. Our memories do not share the same reality as the car or your body. Your imagination about the person who cut you off cannot share the same realness as your car going off the road.

However, and this is the important part to you:

Your sense of certainty about your memories,
and
your sense of certainty about the aroma of the coffee
are the same.

Your sense of certainty does not distinguish between reality and memory. Imagination, memory and reality within the context of certainty, can be experienced as the same.

That is why this next step, Step 4, Journeying To "That Place" is so critical to the process.

STEP 4

Journeying To "That Place"

A famous sculptor was asked how he was able to carve such a lifelike horse out of a block of marble. His reply was, "I simply took away all of the marble that hid the horse." This is essentially, what you do when you journey to "that place." You take away from your experience of reality everything that you can doubt. What remains has to be real.

The process of going to "that place" involves withdrawing the sense of absolute certainty from different focuses of the conscious mind. The mind seeking certainty uses the cosmological screen with its core issue and core beliefs to define what is real in three key areas.

That which is external to the body and the mind
Everything Outside

That which is internal to the mind
Thoughts

That which is internal to the body
Physical Sensations and Feelings

The process used to withdraw the sense of absolute certainty is a very simple one. All that you have to do is to create a sufficient amount of doubt about the reality of what you are focusing on. A sufficient amount of doubt is reached when you are physically and emotionally uncomfortable with the possibility that what you thought was real may no longer be real.

E. Jack Lemon

There are four areas from which you will <u>drain</u> the sense of certainty and a fifth that is imaginary:

- Unconscious *immersion** in the external world
- Conscious immersion in the external world
- Conscious immersion in thoughts
- Trusting the body
- Sensory deprivation tank (imaginary exercise)

Once you have drained/removed the absolute sense of certainty from these areas, you are in a position to experience the truth of these three statements:

I am not the thought; I am the thinker.
I am not the perception; I am the perceiver.
I am not the emotion; I am experiencing the emotion.

The perspective from these three statements gives you the "space" or "separateness" to know that you <u>exist</u> and are <u>experiencing</u> life. In other words, "you are living through your life rather than living in it." The "you" that is the thinker is free to know your core truth.

This challenging of reality usually begins with the external, and moves to the internal mind, then to the body, and finally to imagining you are in a sensory deprivation tank with no stimulus coming into the brain

The conscious mind, when it feels threatened, will willingly shift its focus when the suggestion is made to do so.

---

* Immersion is to be fully associated or identified with the Cultural Cosmology. This identification is so complete that one is not aware of any separation. When you are immersed the statement," You are the thinker; not the thought," makes no sense.

This process of chasing the mind's focus further and further back into itself ends in the mind's recognizing it cannot be certain of anything.

The suggestion is then made to the conscious mind that there is a place it can go where doubt does not exist. This is a place where you are aware that <u>you are thinking</u>, but not concerned with <u>what</u> you are thinking.

The experience of "that place" is entirely personal. The one thing that the mind knows in "that place," is that it exists. The certainty of this truth is so self-evident that contradiction or challenge is impossible. You know you exist because you are aware you are thinking. The only existence beyond this place is oblivion.

Oblivion by definition is a place of non-awareness. If you are not aware, then you cannot be aware of thinking. If you are not aware of thinking, you have no way of determining if you exist. You may exist in oblivion, but you have no way of knowing it.

You now have chased the mind's awareness of itself back as far as it can go. In doing this you have provided the mind with that, for which it has always yearned, the experience of certainty. This experience of a new foundation and definition of itself can be so profound that the mind begins to reorganize itself.

The process for creating doubt can be Socratic in nature, that is to say, a question is asked; an answer is given, and a new question is created out of the answer.

This is the reason a sincere answer is necessary. It is important that you take the question seriously; therefore, search diligently for an honest answer. The questions are designed to create doubt and continue until doubt becomes real. It is by consciously focusing on both the question and the answer, that the mind becomes uncomfortable and wishes to withdraw to a different area where certainty still exists.

Techniques For Creating Doubt When Working Alone

Another way of describing what you are trying to accomplish through doubt is cognitive dissonance. This means that you are trying to create conflict within the mind. When you are working alone, the only technique that you have available to you is self-talk.

Some of my clients have tried to develop strategies and record them. The problem they keep encountering is that the mind is so quick and devious that it out flanks the recording, rendering it clumsy and ineffective.

Here are some tips that we have found to be helpful:
- Make sure you answer fully and take seriously the question you ask yourself.
- Think of the voice that is asking you questions as the interrogator or therapist and the voice that is answering the questions as you.
- Play with making the interrogator's voice louder or firmer than the respondent's voice.
- Play with making the interrogator's voice male or female.
- Play with the intonation of the interrogator's voice as well as speed of delivery.

In other words, make as sharp and clear a distinction between the two voices as you can.

All of the following strategies can be used by yourself or with another person helping you.

Strategies For Creating Doubt Or Cognitive Dissonance

These strategies are just simple examples that can provide a guideline for you if you have the honor of working with someone and helping him get to "that place." When I say guideline, I mean specifically that. I encourage you to use your own language and vocabulary so that you feel comfortable in this process. Also, feel free to make up your own strategies. Creating and developing your own strategies based on what the person is saying is probably going to be more effective than using a script.

Remember each individual has his own cosmological screen. Because of this, you cannot know in advance what strategy will work effectively.

It is also important that you not be afraid of causing the other person harm. The intent is to make him physically and emotionally uncomfortable not to "freak him out." It has been my experience that if a person becomes too uncomfortable, he aborts the process. I have also found that it is helpful if you know the person well enough to have a sense of where his limitations are.

I would encourage you to trust your intuition as you encourage and challenge the other person's mind. Understand that the other person's mind will defend what it calls reality. If you are not successful the first time, analyze what you learned about the other person's mind and plan some questions that will be more successful next time. It is sometimes helpful for me to treat this as a strategy game where I am challenged to outthink the other person's mind. Though the intent is serious, it never hurts to have fun.

E. Jack Lemon

1. UNCONSCIOUS IMMERSION -
IN THE EXTERNAL WORLD

Exercise one

Focusing on the unconscious immersion in the external world means to have the person simply be aware of what is going on around him without being engaged in it. An example would be, to have him just be aware of the room he is sitting in. Encourage the person to have his eyes open during this exercise.

Begin the process by asking this question:

"How do you know that what you perceive right now is not a dream that you are having, while you lie in bed?"

It is important that you insist that the person pursue the question until he recognizes he cannot find an answer. Pursuit continues until he is uncomfortable.

If he is one of those people who has no problem believing that what he perceives is not real, then asks him this question:

" If this is a dream then where is the dreamer?"

Again, pursue the answer to the question until he is uncomfortable.

Exercise two:

Remember a time when you were busy doing something; you may or may not have been with other people. What you are looking for is a memory when you were so busy and so involved that you lost track of time. When you look back on that memory, you are not certain of what

23 to Cone

left onto Cone

Ann Arbor Rd, right

$\frac{1}{2}$ mile left in Ostrander

Dundee Azalia right

$\frac{1}{2}$ mil

right side

you were doing at any given moment. Yet, you were aware of what you were doing, but even that awareness tends to be a bit fuzzy. Examples of this would be unconsciously driving the car, totally immersed in a movie or losing track of time while doing a repetitious task.

This focus of awareness has some unique aspects, which could be described as living unconsciously in the "real world."

- You are totally immersed but unaware of being immersed.
- Body and mind are reacting to thoughts in a dynamic interplay between external world and mind.
- There is little or no awareness of the positions being separate.

Ask the person:

"How did he know what was real during that time of unconscious immersion?"

Whatever his answer, ask him to prove it to himself.

When the person demonstrates physical or emotional discomfort, he should be invited to move to the next area of awareness.

2. CONSCIOUS IMMERSION-
IN THE EXTERNAL WORLD

sharing love

The focus of conscious immersion in the external world is having the person be aware of when he was actively engaged with the world around him. Examples are conversation, sporting events, or ~~making~~ love. Encourage the person to have his eyes open during this exercise.

Exercise one
Say to the person:

"Imagine that you are having an intense conversation with another person. The topic that you are discussing is important to you, and it is important that you make the other person see your point of view."

Say to the person:

"When you critically examine this remembered time, you will discover at least two things.
    1. *You were only half listening to what the person was saying, because you were already formulating your response based on what you knew he was thinking.*
    Question: Is there any way you can know with certainty what the other person was thinking or feeling? "

Remind him that he does not have the power of telepathy.

    2. *"There was a sense of certainty about the rightness of your position.*
    Question: What was that sense of certainty based on?"

Remind him that no matter how absolutely certain he is, absolute certainty is a belief of a cosmological screen.

Ask him:

"What was real during this time of conscious immersion?"

When the person demonstrates physical or emotional discomfort, invite him to move to the next strategy.

Exercise two

People believe that the world around them is how they perceive it. Questions that cause them to examine this assumption can also create cognitive dissonance.

Example 1
Ask him:
"Have you ever seen the full moon? "

When he says, yes, explain to him that technically that is not possible. Whenever he sees the moon, he is actually seeing where it was. The light from the moon takes approximately four and one half seconds to travel from the surface of the moon to your eyes. This means that by the time we see the moon, it has in reality moved. It is impossible for anyone on the earth to see the moon. We can only see it through history.

Example 2
Ask him:
"Have you ever touched something? "

When he says yes, explain to him that technically that is not possible. When we say that we touch something, we are assuming that we are touching it right now. In fact, there is a minor delay from that time your fingers actually touch something to when you recognize it. It takes a certain amount of time for the nerve impulse to travel up the arm and into the brain. It also takes a certain amount of time for the brain to process the information and give that feedback back to the hand. The fact that we ignore these time delays does not deny their reality. We assume that what we experience happens when we experience it. In fact we are always living in a time delay.

If the person argues that, these examples are nonsense and have nothing to do with the real world, remind him that the definition of reality includes what is, not what was.

Ask him:
"To take a moment and seriously consider the fact that he is always living and experiencing the world through a time delay.

Invite him to focus his attention on the world around him and sincerely be aware that he is not experiencing reality but the history of reality. "

When the person demonstrates physical or emotional discomfort, invite him to move to the next area of awareness.

.

3. CONSCIOUS IMMERSION-
IN THOUGHTS

Focusing on conscious immersion in thoughts is to have the person just be aware that he is thinking. Help him focus on the reality of what he is thinking. Encourage the person to have his eyes open during this exercise.

Say to the person:

"Now just pay attention to your thoughts. It does not matter what your thoughts are about; the fact that these are your thoughts allows you to feel quite certain that they are truthful and real."

Say to the person:

"Remember that you have a cosmological screen made up of a core issue and core beliefs. How do you know whether or not your thoughts are in fact accurate or true, since they have been edited even before you speak them?"

Tell him:

"Notice how difficult it is to continue thinking about one thing for very long."

Invite him:

"To try to focus on one thing and pay attention to how soon his mind shifts to something else. "

Ask him:

"How much control does he think he really has over the accuracy and duration of his thoughts?"

Ask him:

"Is there is anything about his thoughts that he can prove is real and factual? How does he know?"

Ask him:

"If he is certain his thoughts are real, where do they exist? Anything that is real must exist somewhere. Another criterion for reality is that another person can verify the objects existence. Can anyone else see, hear, or experience his thoughts? If someone cannot, then how can he prove his thoughts are real?"

When the person demonstrates physical or emotional discomfort, invite him to move to the next area of awareness.

4. TRUSTING THE BODY

Focus the person's awareness on his body, helping him to shift his attention to what his body is feeling at this moment. Encourage the person to have his eyes open during this exercise.
Say to the person:

"If you cannot be certain of the truthfulness or the realness of your thoughts, then surely you can trust the sensations of your body to be real."

Ask him:

"Can you, put your awareness into your body? Are you aware of the pressure of the chair on your body? What about the shoes on your feet?"

Explain to him that:

"When he critically analyzes the interpretations of the sensations that his mind receives from his five senses, he will discover that his body is not doing the feeling, it is his mind. The skin, ears, or eyes are really sensors for the brain and the mind interprets the sensations that the brain receives. These interpretations of the mind are subject to his cosmological screen; therefore, they are edited rather than authentic."

Remind the person:

"That all of his senses can be tricked or fooled. Examples of this would be optical illusion or ghost pain"

Remind him that:

"He <u>cannot</u> be absolutely certain that the perceptions he has about his body, as well as, perceptions he receive from his body are accurate, authentic, or real."

Also remind him that:

"All judgments he has about his body, and all conclusions he has about his body, are edited by his cosmological screen. They are, therefore, interpretations not accurate representations of reality. The cosmological screen cannot distinguish the difference between reality and its interpretation of reality."

When the person demonstrates physical or emotional discomfort, invite him to move to the next area of awareness.

5. SENSORY DEPRIVATION TANK

The purpose of this imaginary exercise is to create within the mind the possibility of its existence without any connection with its body or the outside world. Without new stimuli, all the mind has are memories and the thoughts about these memories. This is usually very uncomfortable for people. The unconfortableness causes the mind to seek any place other than this imaginary tank. This exercise is most effectively done with the person's eyes closed.

Say to the person:

"Imagine that you are in a sensory deprivation tank. This is a tank where you are floating in liquid that has the same density as your body. Your eyes are blocked as well as your ears, and there is sterile air blowing into the mask that covers your head. There are no sensations coming into the brain from the body. Also imagine that you have been in the tank for six hours and you do not know if and when you will leave the tank. The only material the mind has to work on is memories. Imagine a reality where the only thing that is real is your memories. Since you know all of your memories are edited to fit your cosmological screen, how would you know what is real?"

It is important, to allow the person sufficient time to explore the implications of being in the sensory deprivation tank. The more real the experience becomes, the more uncomfortable the person will be.

If the person states that this is a wonderful experience and he would like to stay here forever, try this strategy.

Say to the person:

"A consequence for staying there forever is that you will never feel anything again. You will never taste or see anything again. How does it feel to know that you will never experience anything ever again? How would you know you are alive? "

When the person demonstrates physical or emotional discomfort, say to him:

X *"Is this uncomfortable? There is a place you can go when you*
X *are tired of being uncomfortable. There is place that exists and always has existed. It is where you were shortly after you were born. Some people say this is the place you go to right after you die.*

This place is where you are aware that you are thinking but not paying any attention to what you are specifically thinking. This place may be above your thoughts, behind them, or below them. I cannot know where it is for you, but it does exist.

Ask yourself this question; Since you are in this tank, how do you know you still exist? You know you exist, because you are aware that you are thinking. I am not talking about what you are thinking about, but rather the very fact that you are thinking. Let your mind go looking for this old and familiar place."

When the person demonstrates physical or emotional discomfort, say to him:

"When you arrived at this place that is quiet and comfortable, just be there for awhile. You will notice that this is a place where all that you can be certain of is that you are aware that you are thinking. You might gently be aware that now you have an obvious and self-evident definition of certainty and reality. You cannot get any further back into yourself. If you cease to think or be aware, then you do not exist."

"THAT PLACE"

When the person's body indicates to you that he may have arrived at "that place,"

Ask him:

"What are you aware of?"

If he answers or says nothing, ask him:

"Who is there with you"?

Any kind of answer that communicates to you that the only thing he is aware of is himself indicates that he is in "that place." It is important to check his body language and breathing to confirm this. If he is in "that place" his voice will be quiet and calm, his body will be relaxed, and his breathing will be deep and slow.

While he is in this place, ask him:

"Is your core issue possible?"
(It may be helpful to state for him his core issue.)

His answer should communicate to you that it is not.

Ask him to:

"Say your core truth aloud."

Ask him:

"Is this true?"

His answer should communicate to you that it is.

123

Ask him:

"Are you certain?"

His answer should communicate to you that he is.

Be sure to pay attention to his voice inflection, body language, and breathing as he answers these questions. If he is in "that place," the only change will be a smile or a giggle as you talk to him.

For some people observing themselves thinking is easy. The mind slips into that place like a salmon returning to its home stream. For others, especially those who are very rational, it can be difficult.
Some of the strategies that can be used to assist them are

- Encouraging them not to pay attention to what they are thinking but to step back and observe that they are thinking. (For reasons that I am not sure of, spatial language such as back, up, looking down, in front of, or creating space between, seems to be helpful).
- Explain to them that the place they are trying to get to is not new. This place is where they came from shortly after they were born. It has always been with them. When they were little, all that they knew existed was themselves. There was something outside of them, but they could not be sure of what it was. The only thing they were certain of was that they were.
- Some of my clients have described their interpretation of that place as being in their soul. I have found this imagery to be helpful with my clients who are religious.
- If the person believes in reincarnation then it is helpful to describe "that place" as the awareness

the self has in between lives. This is a space where there is no cosmological screen and there is no body, yet there is still thinking.

These are strategies I have found to be helpful. The most important tool to help someone get to "that place" is cognitive dissonance. When the mind experiences a sufficient amount of conflict and confusion over something that it thought was real, it wants to find some place where it can feel safe from confusion.

The single most determining factor, as to whether a person can easily get to "that place" or not, is his willingness to experience sufficient levels of cognitive dissonance or doubt. If the dissonance is great enough, the body will reflect it and the mind will readily change its focus of attention.

It cannot be stated strongly enough that the mind hates and fears real confusion. It will seek a path away from it. The mind will eagerly accept directions to a place of certainty.

Both the person, who is helping you, and you will know when you have arrived at that place because the mind and body are at peace.

In this place of quiet certainty, a person realizes that the core issue is not wrong, it is simply impossible.

He also realizes when he states his core truth that it is obvious and self-evident. He knows beyond any doubt or contradiction that this is who he truly is and always has been.

This experience is so truly authentic and singular that the mind begins the process of reconstructing the structure through which it has viewed itself in the world. This structure, however, is not a screen, but an emerging Spiritual Cosmology that is based on one's core truth that is unshakable and certain. The mind has been given

what it always desired that is, a place where the mind can know who it is and what the world is.

This reconstruction will take place over time. The conscious mind will become aware of the reconstruction by being surprised with new thoughts and unexpected conclusions. This reconstruction process takes place in an inconsistent fashion, because it is transmutational rather than transformational. That this process is gradual and to some degree unconscious was the confirmation for me, that the process was authentic and real. If the change were to occur rapidly, it would throw the body and the mind into confusion because of the habitual patterns of beliefs that still exist.

My clients report to me that they are having new thoughts about familiar situations. They are also experiencing new or less intense emotions. That is not to say that everyone experiences a smooth transition from his cosmological screen to a perspective that is now grounded in his core truth. Some uncomfortable experiences of this transition will be described in the next section entitled The Fog.

It is important to note that from this experience of knowing, there are two unintended outcomes that can occur:

- You know for certain that the only thing that truly exists in your world is you. You are a class of one. There is no one or no thing to which you can be compared. The only possible feeling you can have for you, is to love you, because you are all that you know for certain exists. Because you know with indisputable proof that you are lovable and acceptable, any core issue that says you are not is simply not true.

- When you are in this space of knowing *the only thing you can be certain of is that you are thinking,* you are also in the doorway to experiencing the

strange sentence

"now." The "now" is living in the present moment with awareness. As you journey to this place more frequently and it becomes familiar, there can come a time when the present moment will break through and you will know with absolute certainty that you are a part of everything that is.

The Process Of Returning

From this position of being in "that place" and knowing for certain what is real (your core truth) one can travel outward visiting each level of awareness (body then thoughts and then external) and assigning to each level a degree of certainty with which you will now be comfortable. Notice how the degree of certainty is lessened the further you travel out from "that place" to the external world.

Edward, Sara, and Elizabeth went to "that place" using variations of the above process. Remember, what I have given you is a guideline. Please do not use it as a script and then wonder why it does not work. You and your partner have minds that can intuitively think and respond. Do not ignore hunches or moments of inspiration while you are in the process. Above all, do not give up.

I have not worked with a person yet who could not get there. It is just easier for some than for others. What seems to determine whether it is easy or not is the language and images used to create the cognitive dissonance and a willingness to experience cognitive dissonance.

Edward

Edward had a relatively easy time getting to "that place." It may have been easier for him for two reasons: one, I had developed, over time, skills in asking questions and two, because he had spent most of his life trying to be somebody other than himself. Whatever the reason, he showed appropriate levels of unconfortableness at each level and was relieved when he got to "that place."

One other factor may have played a part in his easy journey through the process. Edward's primary leaning modality is kinesthetic or body learning. He knows he has learned something when it "sinks in" or "feels solid."

This style may make it easier to move through the process because you move from one focus to another when you are physically and emotionally uncomfortable. Edward is very aware of his body and his discomfort.

When Edward stated his core truth, while he was in "that place" it was with quiet assurance and confidence. Edward knew beyond any doubt that, "I am me."

Sara

Sara also was able to reach "that place" without a great deal of difficulty. It would be more accurate to say that she reached "that place" easily after I figured out what voice to use with her. Sara's primary modality is audio. She pays more attention to what she hears than what she feels or sees. Unfortunately, my speaking voice was the problem. This was revealed when we were discussing why she could not get to "that place."

My voice reminded her of her husband, and as she later stated,"I do not take orders from any man, especially my husband." How I was phrasing the questions communicated to her that I was giving her orders rather than directions. This, plus the similarity between her husband's voice and mine made it difficult for her take direction from me.

We then explored how to solve this dilemma. I asked her, "If there was some voice that she could take direction from." She said she knew only one person's voice that would work, her Sansei or teacher of marital arts. One of the ways Sara kept in shape was through training in marital arts. Sara is currently a 1st. degree black belt. It turns out that when I "coached" her in what to say to herself and had her self-talk be in the voice of her Sansei, it was easy for her.

Another surprise was "that place" turned out to be similar if not exactly the place Sara was taught to go to when she prepared to begin a series of moves. The Sensei described it as a place of quiet and power, where all that exists is you and the moves you are about to make. This is as good a description of "that place" as any other. Sara stated her core truth with a child's smile while she was in "that place." It was stated not so much as a declaration, as a long forgotten truth. Sara knew that, "I am loveable."

Elizabeth

Elizabeth had the most difficulty of the three. It took three sessions and a great deal of discussion before she was finally able to experience "that place." In retrospect, there were three main obstacles.

- Elizabeth is primarily a visual person. She pays attention to what she sees in the world and in her mind. Her mind thinks quickly and evaluates the reasonableness of what she sees and then moves on to the next "picture" or thought. The speed with which she does this made it very difficult to slow her down enough to experience feelings in her body. This rapid movement from one thought to another also kept her from feeling negative emotions.

- Elizabeth was not sure that her life was all that bad. She was not sure that she wanted to change it by "monkeying around" with how she experienced it. She had survived all these years by keeping moving, and it had "worked so far." When I gave her permission to have this view and suggested that we terminate our relationship, she said she would think about it. After a number of weeks, she called me back and said she wanted to try this process because her husband "had just about had it with her."

- Elizabeth has also isolated herself from her family and friends because of her "moving on" strategy. The idea that she could find a place that was permanent and immovable was beyond her experience. In her world being stationary was being vulnerable. This core belief was a consequence of her sexual abuse.

Elizabeth was finally able to experience "that place" by her imagining that there was a time when she was safe and happy; that time was when she was very little before her abuse occurred. She used her granddaughter as a model and "piggy backed" on the image of this small child.

From this perspective, Elizabeth was able to slow down her thoughts and experience the discomfort in her body and mind. Her response to experiencing "that place" was joyful and when she stated her core truth, her voice rang in the office. It was not a shout. It was a declaration of truth, the truth that, "I am."

As you can see from Edward, Sara, and Elizabeth's journeys to "that place, " every person's journey is different. I have had some who could get there by themselves. Others I have helped, and still others have been helped by friends. There is no script, but hopefully you have been given enough information to travel there yourself.

Let me reiterate, "that place" is where you experience yourself as existing apart from what you are experiencing. It is a perspective where you know for certain that:

I am not the thought; I am the thinker.
I am not the perception; I am the perceiver.
I am not the emotion; I am experiencing the emotion.

Because you know this to be true, any self-identity that is social (needing someone or something else) is a lie. As Sara said when she was in "that place," "There is only me here, how can I not love myself?"

You have now gone through the first four steps. This is the most difficult part of the process. In many ways, this is just the beginning. I once discovered from a friend and former teacher, Wayne, that illumination is *discuss* overrated because everyone thinks that it is the end goal, when it is just the beginning. Where you go from here demonstrates the wisdom of his saying. It has been my experience that if you consciously do nothing with what you have experienced, it will slowly over time dissolve your cosmological screen.

However, if you want to act on your new learning, there are some things that you can do.

Step 5 talks about Developing Your Spiritual Cosmology. I would like to suggest that finding others who are taking the same journey is very helpful. It is helpful for a number of reasons: support, common language, shared storytelling, and sharing perspective are just a few. Since people must discover their own spirituality, having or building a community gives you a place to celebrate the experience of a larger inclusive spirituality, sometimes called Mitakuye oyas' in (all are my relatives / we are all interconnected).

STEP 5

Developing A Spiritual Cosmology

The reason I call what replaces the Cultural Cosmology and the cosmological screen, a Spiritual Cosmology, rather than reality cosmology or some other term, is because the primary foundation for living, has become what you know is real. Because you have experienced your realness, you now have access to the realness of creation.

When I, out of the realness that I truly am, relate to the universe that truly is, this is being spiritual. A cosmology that has Mitakuye oyas' in (all are my relatives) as its core does not need a screen or any other person's validation.

The irony is that the culture teaches us that we are a part of the family of man and we feel alone. The experience of being ultimately alone, going to "that place," reveals to us that it is impossible for us to be alone, because we are a part of the greater reality that is creation.

This does not mean that because you have experienced your core truth in "that place" you have been somehow born-again and you and creation are best buddies. This process is transmutational and will continue for the rest of your life.

An excellent symbol for transmutation is a snake shedding its skin. A snake knows when it is time to shed its skin; when that which is inside, is too big for that which is on the outside. The snake removes its skin by rubbing it against its environment. Sometimes it comes off in one piece but other times it tears off in strips.

The power of the snake metaphor, for me, is that the skin underneath looks exactly like the skin that was removed. All of the changes that took place in the snake's growth were inside of him. To the outside world, the snake looks the same just maybe a little bigger.

This is exactly what happens to a person who discovers that he is real. To the world, that person looks the same, but that person views the world and himself quite differently.

The development of a Spiritual Cosmology occurs at the unconscious level, but it can be augmented at the conscious level. This is done through being aware:

- of the "knowings" that are emerging
- it is a developmental process
- the need for using rational thought that is rooted in the core truth

I do not know another word for knowings. They are concepts, definitions, or interpretations that grow out of your core truth. They are not things you believe rather they are things that you know. Knowings are personally self-evident and do not need confirmation or validation from the culture.

Developmental process means that something starts small and over time grows into something larger. The development of the Spiritual Cosmology begins with the core truth out of which grows knowings. These knowings become the framework out of which you interact with the culture and the universe.

The experience of the core truth drains the certainty of the core issue, but it does not destroy it. The core issue, like the core beliefs, is embedded in habitual patterns. These patterns are not just in the mind, they are also imprinted in the body. The mind and the body will dissolve these patterns over time, because they no longer work.

The Fog

For some people, the initial couple of weeks following the experience of "that place" are very uncomfortable. They experience very strong emotions, confusion, and doubt. Several of my clients reported walking around feeling lost and unsure of who they are. Most of my clients reported feelings of being disconnected or unattached.

They also reported that though the anger and confusion were intense, it was almost as if it were happening to someone else. They felt the anger and confusion, but just could not feel attached to them. Others reported that while lying in bed at night, they began to doubt that anything had happened to them; however, they had to make themselves believe that their core issue was true. It no longer felt natural.

The fog does not last for very long, nor does it affect everyone. It is another indication that this process is both powerful and effective. After a few weeks, a person settles down and goes on living his life. The difference is he lives his life more effectively.

Understanding how to process rationally, understanding what the emotional bog is, and having an ever-expanding community of people, who share the same experience, allow you to live through your life rather than to live in it. Because you no longer stay immersed in the Cultural Cosmology, you discover that happiness is no longer an event but rather a consequence of learning to live in reality. One of the most helpful techniques available for the development of the Spiritual Cosmology is rational thought.

So where are Edward, Sara, and Elizabeth now on their journeys? This is obviously an impossible question to answer because they are constructs. However, it may be helpful to see how this process does affect people's lives. To that end, I have created answers to how they are doing. All of the changes demonstrated by Edward, Sara, and Elizabeth are reasonable and reflect the growth I have seen in my clients and myself.

Edward

Edward is evaluating whether he wants to continue working in the public sector and is now open to dating. He is sure, however, that anyone he finds to marry will have to know what her core truth is. He reports that life is lighter and its fun to watch people walking around in their bubbles (his description of a cosmological screen). He is in no hurry to do any of these things. His response to my questions about the future is "I am still developing my Spiritual Cosmology and I want to discover who God is for me before I do anything. God may have information I can use."

Sara

Sara and her husband are exploring sexuality between the two to them. She has decided that her mother has the right to be anything she wants. She has gotten over the guilt she had for not being able to stop her children from having a core issue. She understands now that it is a necessary part of child development. She is committed to helping them find their core truths as soon as they are old enough. This will be interesting for me to watch, because I do not know, what the youngest age is when one can discover his core truth. Sara's relationship with her church and God is undergoing a change and no one knows what the future will manifest.

Elizabeth

Elizabeth's growth has taken the form of developing a deep sense of spirituality. She practices prayer and is exploring being able to see elves and fairies. She saw them when she was a child and is convinced that her cosmological screen blinded her to them. Her relationship with her husband has deepened, especially since he came and discovered his core truth. He has started to go to church with her and is trying to see elves also.

Edward, Sara, and Elizabeth, are in the process of developing their Spiritual Cosmology. This is a lifelong journey.

There is no predicting the future; however, for all of them the future will be better than the past, because they know who they are. They also know there is a creator who is as real as they are. This is not a religious statement. It is a spiritual statement.

It has been my experience that when you discover that you are real, you inevitably discover that the universe is real, as well. The experience of knowing that you are a part of everything that is can be a profoundly healing experience.

We as human beings are taught by experience, that we are alone, separate from everything. We spend a great deal of time and energy trying to overcome that state of isolation. If we are not trying to overcome it, we are trying to cope with our resignation to it. Either way huge amounts of time and energy are spent in distraction and misery.

If you live long enough you will experience many times, what a friend of mine calls, "the 2 a.m. confrontation with yourself." This is when there is no one around; there are no distractions and you feel totally alone.

I believe this experience is universal. I also believe that the only cure is the experience of knowing you belong and are a part of the consciousness that is the universe. This cure is naturally available to anyone who journeys to "that place" and experiences his core truth.

The rest of the book is a resource for you to continue living and developing your Spiritual Cosmology. These resources are broken into three areas:

Answers to some difficult questions
Operational definitions
A Toolbox with Helpful Concepts

The answers to difficult questions are just that. They are my answers to these questions. These answers seem reasonable and real to me at this stage in my growth. You may agree, disagree, or have different answers to these questions. Next year, because of my growth, I may answer them differently. I can know only what is reasonable and real for me now.

The operational definitions are expanded definitions that have developed out of my conversations with my people, clients, and friends. I believe that conversations with people can provide us with the stimulus necessary for continued growth. This is an important reason for people participating in a community that is inclusive, nonjudgmental, and challenging.

The Toolbox and Helpful Concepts are strategies and conceptual awarenesses that my people and I have found helpful. They are helpful when you are in mental conflict especially when you are in the fog. The Toolbox and Helpful Concepts can be signposts and map directions for you. They also can function as reminders of who you are and what is real when you become immersed in the Cultural Cosmology.

The last section of the book consists of implications and thoughts that I believe naturally flow out of the experience of knowing and living your core truth. This section, like the psychotherapeutic description of the journey, is very rational.

It is accurate to say that I do not have faith in God rather that I have knowledge of God.

This knowledge results from the rational processing of my experiencing the "all present universe." My relationship with the universe, which I defined as spiritual, is dynamic and enfolding. That is the reason I entitled this last section "What I know thus far."

Resources For Developing A Spiritual Cosmology

Answering Difficult Questions

In my work as a therapist and as a clergyperson, I am often asked the same questions repeatedly. When I was viewing the world and myself through my cosmological screen, these questions were indeed, difficult, if not impossible to answer.

However, when viewed from my core truth and my developing Spiritual Cosmology, these questions not only have answers, but the answers are reasonable. I do not maintain that these answers are right or true. I do assert, however, that they are reasonable, given my perspective of reality.

I recognized that, "Even if one develops the Spiritual Cosmology as his primary cosmology, the fact remains that one still has to live in the culture whose view of reality is different."

I further stated that, "I would suggest that the resolutions to this conflict are to be found in the transmutations of a Cultural Cosmology into a Spiritual Cosmology. This transmutation would be done out of trial and error, therefore, would be gradual."

It would be an error to conclude from what I have said that I think a Cultural Cosmology is bad or wrong. As I have often stated, "A Cultural Cosmology is a necessary developmental stage of growth whether for an individual or for the human species."

It is a common experience of people who are living out of a Spiritual Cosmology, that they have very few things they know definitively.

141

E. Jack Lemon

    They do have, however, many questions that seem to have reasonable and obtainable answers.

    What follows are questions that have been raised by people who are learning to live in a Spiritual Cosmology. This is not to be considered a definitive list of questions, but it is hoped that they are questions that provide resources for anyone who wishes to discover reality as experienced through a Spiritual Cosmology.

Why have I not experienced
God's forgiving me?

Forgiveness in a Cultural Cosmology

In a Cultural Cosmology, one seeks forgiveness when he has done something that he or other people believe is wrong.

This sense of being wrong is always in relationship to an external power. This authority has been given the power to determine what is right and what is wrong. This power may be present as a parent or the power may be a moral law established by someone who has authority.

In either case one needs to experience the lifting of the guilt, he has experienced and accumulated because of committing this wrong.

The problem for people in a Cultural Cosmology is that they have to believe that this external power can and will forgive them and that they are worthy of forgiveness.

In regard to God as a powerful being, most people have so many contradictory beliefs that the question can or will God forgive me cannot be answered with confidence.

Am I worthy of forgiveness brings a host of issues that many people have as a result of growing up in a culture that believes perfection is possible.

If the contradictory beliefs about God and the interpersonal issues of worthiness were not enough, you face an even more daunting task, which is to decide whether you can trust your conclusions about God and your worthiness.

How does one know that what he believes about God is right? It may be that a specific degree of certainty is necessary in order for one to allow oneself to experience God's forgiveness.

The easiest way to be certain about God is to piggyback on someone else's certainty. This person also would have to be perceived as more powerful than you for the certainty to be effective.

Many people only know that forgiveness is possible because some authority says so. It may also be that when they have an experience that they think is God's forgiving them, that the experience has to be affirmed and validated by the authority before they trust it.

For all of the above reasons it seems reasonable that most people would have difficulty experiencing God's forgiveness.

Forgiveness in a Spiritual Cosmology

The primary need for forgiveness is absent in a Spiritual Cosmology.

You need forgiveness when you have done something wrong. If there are no absolutes to measure right or wrong then a new concept is available. This new concept is growth.

In the context of a Spiritual Cosmology, there is no right or wrong in the absolute sense, but there are consequences for one's action.

Your understanding of the rightness or wrongness of a specific decision or action may very well change as you grow and change your cosmological screen. It is more important within the context of a Spiritual Cosmology to discover what did not work for you and learn from it, than it is to feel the deep need for forgiveness from someone else or yourself.

The reason for this is that you have no way of knowing for <u>certain</u> what the person you "wronged" feels or even if he feels you "wronged" him.

An apology or explanation may be appropriate, but you do not need his forgiveness for you to feel happy.

Also forgiving yourself makes no sense and is unnecessary if you are seeking to learn from your mistake. What is important is that you have learned from the experience.

The guilt in this situation, like that in a trauma, can be released by knowing there are no absolutes. By unhooking the emotions that are attached to the parental imperatives and extracting the lesson from the situation, you are free to continue living and learning.

E. Jack Lemon

Are strong negative emotions an indication that one is currently immersed in a Cultural Cosmology?

The Cultural Cosmology has educated and encouraged us to ask questions in a yes or no format. This format is very efficient if one believes that questions really have definite answers. When one is experiencing the Spiritual Cosmology, definite answers are hard to come by because he realizes that everything depends upon the interpretation of his perspective; therefore, one tends to answer questions using a style that is more reflective than declarative.

Based on the reports from other people, as well as my own experience, the dominant emotion one experiences while being present in the moment is identified as peace, joy, happiness, or love. It may well be that all of these different terms describe the same emotional state.

One of the functions of emotions is to give feedback on your interactions with the outside world. Many people divide emotions into five different states. They are happiness, sadness, anger, fear, and guilt. In the Cultural Cosmology, one of the emotions is positive; the rest are negative.

Psychologists understand that emotions do more than give information to the self about its interactions with the outside world. They also help the memory and internal dialogue fix the memory and conclusions about the interaction.

This reinforcement function is used by the mind in a feedback loop between memory and conclusion to deepen and strengthen this association.

This reinforcement process is one of the foundations of education.

The more powerful the negative emotion, the more likely one is to remember the experience and the conclusion connected to the emotion. This feedback loop of the memory of the experience, the emotion, and the conclusion, support the process for education. It is in fact a major part of the mechanism of "does it work."

A subtle presupposition in the above process is, if I feel the same way about the memory today as I did when it happened then, it must be true. This presupposition is so convincing and reasonable that it often goes unexamined.

Close examination of the presupposition, if I feel the same way about the memory today as I did when it happened, it must be true, reveals that this is not the only conclusion one can draw from the feedback loop.

It may be more accurate to say that the reason we feel the same today as when it happened is that we have not grown in our perspective. After all, the event, which is held in memory and reinforced by emotion and conclusion, has no existence outside of our mind. Since we know that memories are created from a certain point of view and that a certain point of view affects the conclusion, we are free to question the truth of the memory and conclusion.

Since memories are fixed in part by strong negative emotions connected to specific conclusions and a feedback loop reinforces our belief that the memory is true and accurate, then strong negative emotions, especially when they are connected to memories, keep us in the Cultural Cosmology.

We are convinced our memories are factual. We are, therefore, convinced that our factual memories are real and have power over us.

It would be accurate to say, that any emotion that is experienced as undesirable, is a strong indication that you are immersed in the Cultural Cosmology.

How can I get over past traumas, when I feel the same way today as I did when it happened?

A Cultural Cosmology's perception of trauma

A trauma is a significant negative experience. This negative experience may be one event or a series of interconnected events that communicate the same negative message. This significant negative experience was interpreted in a very specific manner. This manner was that something was done to you over which you had little or no control. Someone or thing exercises power over you and you are helpless to stop or resolve it.

The irony of trauma is, it is not the event that ultimately causes the damage, so much as the ongoing negative internal dialogue that deepens and integrates the message of responsibility and injury.

Inherent in the experience of trauma is the aspect of responsibility and its accompanying concept, blame. These two powerful concepts fix our point of view and interpretation of the event. They do not allow for any other perspective because we believe that our memory is not an interpretation, but the literal truth. We know and maybe fear beyond any contradiction that the videotape in our mind is accurate and factual.

This true perspective cannot be changed unless the facts change and since this happened in the past, it is obvious that the facts cannot and never will be modified.

The only conclusion you can draw is that you have been damaged in some way and it may be your fault. You cannot heal from this damage since it was done to you; therefore, you will have to try to get along as best you can.

You can try to forget it or hide from it, but you know the damage will always remain. A common strategy for "getting along in life" is to repress the memory. This enables you to ignore the cause of the pain, while allowing the trauma to affect your attitude and behavior.

A Spiritual Cosmology's perception of trauma

A Spiritual Cosmology recognizes that something happened to you and that it was a negative experience.

This cosmology allows asking interesting and informative questions about the experience. It does not try to assign blame, rather helps you to discover what you have learned from the experience.

It is through acknowledging and integrating the growth one has harvested from the trauma that enables one to let go of the past.

Letting go of the past quite literally means to unhook the emotions from the memory. Discovering what absolute rule, you have violated, does this. These rules are almost always coached in parental imperatives such as should have, must have, or ought to have.

When you recall your mind to the present and remember that the only thing that is real is your interpretation of your perception then the parental imperatives, lose power. Without the power to support the judgment, the emotion disappears in the light of reality. Without the emotion to anchor the memory, the video-tape of the experience can and will fade away.

E. Jack Lemon

What can I do? I feel trapped.
I do not know how to get out
of the situation I am in.

The short answer is to think about what is real and what is imaginary. One of the joys of the Spiritual Cosmology is that one can know and experience reality. From this perspective, those things that are imaginary are easy to see, hear, and feel.

The question, "What is real in this situation?" is often helpful when we find ourselves immersed in the emotional bog of imagination. Just to ask ourselves the question what do I see or hear or feel is not enough; we must also add the concept of reality to the question. The power of this question is evident once one has experienced the Spiritual Cosmology.

But even if one has not experienced a Spiritual Cosmology, defining what you know for fact is a helpful first step leading you out of the perceived trap.

If you were to take a videotape of your situation and use only the video portion of the tape not the sound, what would you see? It is highly improbable that you would see any kind of trap at all. Rather you would see people interacting with each other. Your ability to draw conclusions based only on the tape would be limited.

This videotape, without the audio, is closer to reality than all of the imagined obligations, dependencies, and pain that you are experiencing. Just because the voices in our minds sound real and feel real, does not mean that they are real.

Even though you think you know what another person feels and thinks about you, and even though you believe you can predict his actions, and his actions will cause you great pain, you do not and cannot know what he thinks or will do except in probabilities.

150

It is a truism that no one can make us think feel or do anything we do not choose to think, feel or do.

What we are saying to ourselves when we feel trapped is that there are no other alternatives. We believe that we know exactly how the future will play out if we choose one course of action over another. We also believe that we know exactly how we and the other person will think, feel, and respond. We are also afraid of the pain we know we will experience because of the action we will take. We are so confident in the accuracy of our knowledge and predictions that we have rendered ourselves immobile.

It is not enough that we cannot act, but we are also full of fear, rage, and guilt. What has just been described is an emotional bog of imagination. This emotional bog of imagination can be dispelled very quickly by deciding to focus on what is real.

It is a fact that whatever you decide, will have consequences, but it is not a fact that you can know and predict exactly what those consequences will be. You also cannot know or predict with any certainty how you will feel or respond to those consequences.

It is important to remember that the only thing that is real is your interpretation of your perspective. If you find a way to change your interpretation, of your perspective, your feelings, and responses can and will be quite different from what you imagine.

This is not to say that the consequences will be necessarily positive. Nevertheless, you do know that whatever the consequences are, you will not be destroyed, harmed, or wounded unless you choose to be. Since you are the only thing that exists for sure in your world, why would you choose to destroy, harm, or wound yourself?

One of the other benefits from asking the question about what is real is that if you can experience even for just a moment the reality of the Spiritual Cosmology, you will see your situation dramatically different. The walls of the trap disappear; the chains fall away, and the terrible weight is lifted from you shoulders and heart. The reason they disappears so quickly is that they never existed in reality only in your bog of imagination.

Why do I believe that I am not good enough, or powerful or significant when my mind tells me these are not true?

There are many ways you could frame this question depending on what psychological, religious, or scientific school you support. I will try to answer this question using the metaphor of a tree. The trunk of a tree is your core issue and the branches are the many core beliefs that evolve out of the core issue.

Core issue and core beliefs

A core issue is an I-am… statement that the mind makes to the self at a very early age. It is the structure of your early cosmological screen. This I-am statement will determine the point of view, from which you will view yourself, and your interactions with the world.

This statement is a conclusional statement based on the mind's interpretation of who it is, who the world is, and how they are interacting with each other.

This conclusional statement is not based on fact but on one's interpretation of the facts. Once this statement is in place, the mind builds on it through editing and interpreting new experiences so that they support the conclusional statement.

For most people their whole lives are constructed based on this very early conclusional statement. It is the foundation, the core issue, the trunk of the tree that supports our interpretations of the experiences of our life.

The way the core issue develops this power over of our lives is by growing a series of core beliefs. These beliefs are most often expressed in if-then statements, such as, if I am dumb then I cannot figure things out.

These core beliefs are so familiar and compelling that we do not examine them for truth, because we feel certain that they are true.

The reason we feel certain they are true is that as we look back on our lives we see the cause and effect relationship between our core belief and what happens to us. Human beings' lives thus become truly self-fulfilling prophecies.

Our lives cannot change unless the core beliefs and ultimately the core issue are carefully examined as to whether they are true or not. True, in this situation, simply means are they real.

Real in this situation is defined as verifiable by something other than you. An example of an effective question is, "Can you take a videotape of it without sound and draw the same conclusion?" If you cannot take a video of it and draw the same conclusion then your core issue and core beliefs are not real and are probably irrational. Irrational means made up based on speculation, in other words, not true.

When one discovers that his core issue and core beliefs are untrue, then he is free to create core beliefs that are true. When one substitutes a core truth for a core issue, the whole interpretation of one's life changes. The cosmological screen is profoundly altered and one sees not only the past and present differently, but he discovers he can create a different future.

Many times when one asks the question, "Why do I believe that I am not good enough, or powerful or significant when my mind tells me these are not true?" it feels like we are whining or asking a rhetorical question. With the metaphor of core issue and beliefs, one can now actually attempt to answer this question.

Discovering your core issue and beliefs

Core issues are expressed in I-am statements. If you pay attention to what you say about yourself either when talking to someone else or through self-talk, you will hear statements that begin with I am. Make note of the statements. If you listen carefully, you will notice there is a theme to the statements. If you are fortunate enough to have friends that have known you for a considerable period of time, ask them about the theme of your I-am statements.

Once you have identified the theme of your I-am statements, you can begin to play with the words until you have found the one I-am statement that feels true, is very clear, or sounds right. You may discover when you say the I-am that you feel emotional or it feels certain or it feels scary. If it is your core issue, you will know for certain it is correct, because you and your friends will see you physically respond to the statement.

You now can use a similar process to discover what your core truth is.

When you go to "that place" and experience the reality of your core truth, you realize that none of the negative things you believed about yourself are possible. With this realization, you can discover that you, alone, are responsible for creating the original irrational core issue and beliefs. Since you are responsible for the creation of core issue and core beliefs, you now have the power to change them. When you have gone to "that place" and experienced your core truth, you can experience and create knowings. Knowings are much more powerful and real than core beliefs

Once you have discovered and experienced your core truth, the question, "Why do I believe that I am not good enough, or powerful or significant when my mind tells me these are not true?" will no longer be relevant or

useful. It may remain as a habitual pattern, but it will very quickly lose its power to control you.

You have read my answers to some tough questions. My wish for you is that you give yourself permission to ask hard and complex questions. You know what is real and reasonable for you. Do not be afraid to discover your own answers. Remember, any answer you find will be yours and yours alone. Also, know that no one has the "right" and absolute answer. All answers are contextual and specific for that moment in time. As you grow in you Spiritual Cosmology, watch how your answers change.

My Operational Definitions

I have already explained the differences between a dictionary definition of a word or concept and the operational definition. Many of the definitions for words and concepts in this section begin with a question. The reason for this is that these operational definitions grew out of conversation between my clients and me. My clients have been a valuable resource for me in this whole process. So where appropriate I begin the definition with one of their questions.

◆ Goal Setting

Why do you say,
"Setting goals is a dangerous thing to do?"

Cultural Cosmology
Within the context of a Cultural Cosmology, goal setting is an appropriate and necessary thing to do in order to accomplish anything.

This is a rational strategy when one is immersed in a linear and deterministic world. If you believe that things are a certain way and that cause-and-effect can be known and planned for, then goal setting is an effective strategy.

There are inherent problems with goal setting, however. What do you do and feel when you cannot achieve your goal? For many people there is a sense of failure or inadequacy. Many other people experience regret or anger, because the things they hoped to do after they achieved their goal will now not happen. These negative emotions do not promote a sense of peace and well being.

One other inherent problem with goal setting is that the culture teaches us to focus on the goal.

The belief is that the more you focus on the goal, the greater likelihood it will be accomplished.

When you focus on the goal, you automatically exclude many other things. This may limit your ability to see problems or opportunities. Concerning the fact that focus may increase the likelihood that the goal can be obtained, this only works in a deterministic world where all factors can be accounted for and planned for. Experience teaches us that we cannot know all factors and that many things can happen over which we have no control.

One cannot say with certainty that focusing all your attention and energy on the goal will increase its likelihood of being accomplished.

Take for example this situation: someone offers you $100 if you can spell the word pneumonia correctly. You go to the dictionary and you focus all of your time and attention on discovering how to spell pneumonia. You do not find it in the dictionary so you get a larger dictionary and a still larger dictionary, but you lose the hundred dollars because you still cannot spell it. You become angry and frustrated because of your inadequacies. You did not know and no one told you that pneumonia was spelled with a P not an N.

Spiritual Cosmology

Within a Spiritual Cosmology, it may not make sense to set definite goals, because in reality there are always many unintended outcomes.

It is more effective strategy to set the direction in which one wishes to go without a clearly determined outcome in mind. This allows one to create order in one's life and at the same time to be open to emerging opportunities and lessons.

158

Addicted to Certainty

It has been my experience that the driving force behind a Spiritual Cosmology is growth rather than accomplishment. This driving force of growing takes place within the context of reality so that one does not force the future into a specific form but rather is living into it.

True reality does have order in its movement. This order seems to follow a path of least resistance. It is possible when one is present in reality to perceive and respond to this path. It has been my experience, that by following the path of least resistance, I end up where I would like to be. In fact, most times where I end up is better than where I imagined I would be.

Although the strategy of living into the future by following the path of least resistance seems highly irrational and unproductive when compared to linear goal setting, the result in my life is that, I have been able to accomplish more while having more fun than when I set goals.

This only happens at a certain personal energy field of heightened awareness and balanced state of karma. Subconscious lethargic patterns must have been exspelled. One is moved automatically.
Examples:

✦ Forgiveness

Why is it easier to forgive other people than it is to forgive myself?

The answer to this why question, like so many why questions depends upon your perspective. "Why" questions always have a host of alternative answers rather than just one definitive answer. When one asks a "why" question he is seeking a definitive cause and effect. It may be very difficult if not impossible to find such an answer.

Having said this, let us see if we can find some probable reasons for this common experience. These reasons will all be rooted in a Cultural Cosmology because forgiveness is not mandatory in a Spiritual Cosmology.

If you feel you need to forgive either yourself or someone else, then you have to believe you have broken not just a social but also a moral law. You need to rid yourself of the burden of guilt. If you do not rid yourself of this burden, the memory of the transgression and its associated emotion will become fixed in your memory. Eventually you may believe that it is not possible to get over it.

If you have a core belief that tells you, that you are damaged, worthless, and imperfect or any other similar message, then forgiveness of self is not possible. It does not matter how hard you try or what you do, you believe essentially that you are unforgivable.

Remember, this is a core belief, a foundational brick of your self-identity. It is easy to imagine that other people are not essentially flawed and worthy of forgiveness. You can forgive the other person because the rule of God-given morality insists on forgiveness as a condition of love. Because you are fatally flawed, this rule of forgiveness does not apply to you.

It is also easy to imagine that God could and would forgive you but it is virtually impossible for you to receive God's forgiveness because of your deep belief that you are essentially unworthy.

The only hope you have to receive forgiveness for yourself is for some authority you believe in to tell you that God has forgiven you in spite of your own un-worthiness.

If you seek to forgive yourself, change your core issue to something that allows it to happen, in other words, your core truth. This would allow you to change your cosmological screen to a Spiritual Cosmology. In the Spiritual Cosmology, the need for forgiveness is replaced by a desire to grow.

define grow again

to grow in contentment, joy, creativity, spontaneity, sacred sensitivity

◆ Time

How can you say,
"The self is a moment in time,
when I can see me?"

    The question, "What is the self?" has been asked by human beings since the dawn of awareness. Any definitive answer that you come up with ultimately depends upon your point of view. These points of view can range from scientific to religious. Within the context of these teachings the self is seen from two particular points of view; they are the Cultural Cosmology and the Spiritual Cosmology.

    Our experience in the Cultural Cosmology is that the self is separate and distinct from the world around it, yet interconnected with other human beings in some indistinct and intuitive fashion. *(I question intuitive)*

    Our experience in the Spiritual Cosmology is that any discussion of the self must take into account concepts such as "the present," the unity of all things and the impossibility of defining the self as separate from creation.

    These two points of view have such different assumptions and definitions about the self that a meaningful dialogue between someone who is immersed in a Cultural Cosmology and one who is living out of a Spiritual Cosmology will be extremely difficult.

    It is possible, because your Spiritual Cosmology evolves developmentally out of a Cultural Cosmology, to understand the cultural point of view. It may be impossible for someone with a Cultural Cosmology to understand a Spiritual Cosmological point of view, because he has not experienced this perspective yet.

change sentence to start with Because

This is analogous to someone who knows the basics of mathematics, trying to understand the point of view of algebra before he has been taught it.

It may well be that from a Spiritual Cosmological point of view, the most that can be shared about the self's understanding of the self is: the self is that aspect of consciousness, that is aware its perceptions are the result of its interpretation of reality.

The question, "How can you say that the self is a moment in time when I can see me?" demonstrates this difficulty.

From a cultural perspective, the self is a distinct me while from a spiritual perspective the self lives only in a moment of time. In addition to this from the cultural point of view, the past and future must exist. The past exists as we remember it and the future is controllable through good planning.

From the Spiritual Cosmological point of view, the past does not exist except as a highly edited memory and the future cannot be determined. The only real experience of time that is available to us is the present moment.

Clearly, some questions cannot be adequately addressed unless one knows from which point of view the question arises and to whom the question is addressed.

◆ Antithetical Statements

Why do you say that,
"We can believe antithetical or contradictory statements only as long as those statements remain unexamined?"

Antithetical statements are two statements that are exactly the opposite of each other. Example: one can believe that, "You should look before you leap," and one also can believe that, "He who hesitates is lost." If you have both of these beliefs at the same time, your only real choice is to do nothing.

Our mind is capable of associating two things together without examining whether or not the statements are antithetical. Advertising uses this unique ability of the mind to get us to buy substances that are not good for us. The statement, "Winston tastes good like a cigarette should" was repeated so many times on television and on the radio that many people began to associate Winston cigarettes with good taste.

Reasonable and intelligent people bought cigarettes to smoke even though they knew that the cigarettes could cause lung cancer and emphysema. Even when their experience of smoking showed them that it was dirty and addictive, they responded positively to the picture of Winston cigarettes.

Advertisers are able to utilize this ability because our mind thinks in terms of association without analyzing the truth or reasonableness of the association.

We are capable of believing all manner of contradictory statements. If we say these statements to ourselves often enough, we believe that they are true statements.

If we believe the true statements long enough, they become factual statements and cannot be changed.

An example of this would be the statement, "If you love me, you will try to kill me." This statement is not an imaginary one. One of the people I know carried this belief around with him for almost 50 years. Even when it was pointed out to him by the therapist that the statements were antithetical, they still felt right in his mind and he defended them.

Many of the core beliefs that we have about the world and ourselves are antithetical, therefore, tend to be self-defeating or in the worst case self-destructive. It is very difficult to convince someone that his or her core beliefs are in fact antithetical. The reason for this is that the beliefs feel so true.

Within the context of a Spiritual Cosmology, however, antithetical core beliefs disappear very quickly. When you know through experience that the only thing that is real is your interpretation of your perception and that there are no absolutes, then you have an objective position from which to evaluate whether the core belief is real or not.

In the reality of the Spiritual Cosmology, one does not discover many things that are antithetical. The reason I did not state that there are no antithetical statements in Spiritual Cosmology is because reality is much more complex than I can comprehend.

E. Jack Lemon

✦ Mitakuye oyas'in (all are my relatives)

Why do you say,
"The experience of being a part of the circle of life is different for those in the Spiritual Cosmology than for those in the Cultural Cosmology?"

What you focus on is what you make real. This simple statement is literally true.

In the Cultural Cosmology, we focus on ourselves, or more accurately, we focus on the imaginary world of past–future and the interaction between ourselves and others, who live in our imaginary world.

In the Spiritual Cosmology, which is rooted in the experience of the present moment, we grow to focus on the reality that we are a part of everything. This realty is experienced as unconditional love.

It is easy to focus on the imaginary world of past-future. Almost everything in our culture proclaims the reality of this imaginary world. Our senses are almost continually bombarded by stimulation from either the world or our memory.

Our bodies and our minds unconsciously conspire to keep us preoccupied. The body experiences speed as pleasure, so as the rate of change in our world increases, the body/mind in an addictive response craves more stimulation and novelty.

For many people if they are not doing something, they feel lost. The body/mind also prefers comfort. We often equate comfort with familiarity and predictability. One of the reasons the body/mind prefers comfort is that it is not stressful.

Addicted to Certainty

The irony is that the Cultural Cosmology has set up conditions for the maximum amount of stress.

Our society believes that speed and innovation are necessary for success, while an individual person may believe that the same old thing is necessary for happiness. The body/mind believes both of the statements and moves back and forth between these two poles, trying to find a balance.

Balance can never be achieved, because of the increasing speed of complexity in our society. In response to this imbalance, we focus more and more on the skills and abilities necessary for surviving in our imaginary world. We imagine that these skills and abilities are essential if we are to be happy and successful.

An accurate metaphor for what it is like to live in the 21st century is a treadmill that is increasing in speed. We walk on the treadmill while an imaginary future is being shown on the television in front of us. The closed captioning on this screen declares in bold letters "if you are not a success then you are a failure, and it is your fault."

It is no wonder that many people seek the oblivion that is found in addictions or depression in order to escape.

The reality of the Spiritual Cosmology cannot compete with the unconscious intensity of a Cultural Cosmology. It is only when we become consciously aware of what is actually real and certain that we can find peace and balance.

This awareness must be sought with intentionality. All the classes and all the information about the Spiritual Cosmology are useless without our focusing on the experience of learning and growing.

needs discussion

167

E. Jack Lemon

It is extremely difficult to focus on the Spiritual Cosmology when one is busy responding to all of the important responsibilities we imagine that we have.

When we are living out of the Spiritual Cosmology, we know that all we are responsible for is our interpretations of our perceptions. All other responsibilities are ours by choice.

This truth means that we can remake decisions and choices about our responsibilities. One of the consequences of this may be the releasing ourselves from these responsibilities. Without this burden, it may be easier for us to spend time alone.

Alone, in this context, means withdrawing from the Cultural Cosmology. This may be done by going for a walk, sitting in the midst of nature or any other form of meditation.

Being alone allows us to create space for the experience of the present moment. It encourages us to remember that we are a part of everything that is. It gives us time to see, hear, and feel that the only thing we know for certain is that we exist. It is from this knowledge that a doorway is opened into the reality of what we call God's love.

An easy benchmark for how we are growing in the Spiritual Cosmology is by monitoring how much time do we want to spend being alone and aware. In the beginning, it is easier to be aware of peace when we are alone. The experience of Mitakuye oya s'in is ultimately the experience of peace.

This experience of peace can and will become so desirable, it will be the foundation out of which you live into your future. It will become the basis for your relationships and the interpretation of your perception. You will live easily within the culture because you will truly know what is real.

◆ Hope

Why do you say,
"Hope can be a negative emotion?"

This is another example of how difficult and slippery language can be. How hope is defined within the context of a Cultural Cosmology is profoundly different from how it is defined in a Spiritual Cosmology.

Cultural Cosmology

In the Greek myth of Pandora's Box, after all of the things that would cause humanity to despair were released, what remained in the box was hope. Hope is that which enables us not to succumb to despair. This myth is a delightful description of the function of hope. Hope is the anticipation that someone or something will make the future better.

The problem with this understanding of hope is that it inherently appeals to a power outside of us, and it involves imagining the future in a very specific way. By appealing to an external agent for rescue, it subtly places us in a victim position. In many ways, we are left passively waiting for this improbable event to occur. Knowing that hope resides in the future, it becomes a carrot leading us along the same well-worn path.

Hope provides no direction or strategies to help us accomplish that for which we are hoping. Within the Cultural Cosmology, hope becomes the jailer that maintains the illusion of helplessness.

Hope is often seen as beautiful and necessary. In fact, it does promote survival, although it cannot enable one to achieve peace and happiness.

The reality is that peace and happiness have to be created by the self rather than being provided by something outside the self.

Spiritual Cosmology

The function that hope provides within the Cultural Cosmology is not necessary within a Spiritual Cosmology. When one recognizes that all one has is one's interpretation of one's perspective and that the future cannot be known or predicted in any absolute sense, then merely hoping that something will happen is pointless.

If the only thing that exists is the present and it may or may not be connected to the past or the future, then one is free to do what one can to move into the future one desires. You are free to examine what has not worked thus far. You can ask new questions and plan new strategies. You are in a position to evaluate whether or not your strategies have worked and if they have not, to change strategies.

The probability of achieving what you have hoped for is far greater within a Spiritual Cosmology than within a Cultural Cosmology, because you are not waiting for something to happen, but rather you are actively working toward it.

As one person has put it, hope in the Cultural Cosmology can be seen as anticipating there is a light at the end of the tunnel. Whereas hope in the Spiritual Cosmology sees the light and knows there is an end to the tunnel.

- Note I am aware that I used the word hopefully in the text of the book. Another word would not accurately communicate my intent, in other words hopefully *works for me.*

170

◆ Emotional Bog

Why do I feel more emotionally screwed up now than I did before going to "that place?"

Once you have experienced "that place" where you know with certainty that you exist, then you also know with certainty that there is an *observer** and there is that which is being observed.

This perspective is difficult to maintain especially in the beginning development of the Spiritual Cosmology. This level of awareness does not remove the trappings of a Cultural Cosmology such as sequential time, predictable cause and effect, and powerful negative emotions.

We are social creatures; therefore, we maintain a kind of dialogue with the world and ourselves. This dialogue is supported and maintained by the Cultural Cosmology.

Emotions play an important part in this dialogue. Our core issue presupposes there is something outside of ourselves that is more powerful and real than we are. We must be connected to whatever is outside of ourselves. We accept the self-judgment that results from this connection and spend the rest of our lives stuck in an emotional bog trying to resist the self-imposed verdict.

We do not realize that much of the time we live in an emotional bog. The emotional bog carries with it connotations that are not pleasant; however, for many people the emotional bog is the only life they know and it is neither pleasant nor unpleasant; it is the way life is.

---

* Observer is a descriptive label for watching the world from a position of knowing you exist.

It is important to recognize where one is, before one can change.

Once one has discovered the impossibility of his core issue and installed a new I-am statement, the brain will begin to modify the cosmological screen; however, one still has a lifetime of habitual patterns.

These patterns of emotional associations still can be triggered and experienced. It is important to have strategies that enable you to recognize when you are in the bog and how to get out of it.

One of the most powerful strategies is to take a moment to experience your core truth.

One of the most effective strategies is to remember that emotions are a reaction to an interpretation of reality rather than being the validation of reality. I am not the perception; I am the perceiver

The strategy that I use the most is simply to remind myself that the experience of the emotional bog will soon pass.

◆ Wounding

Why do you say,
"Immersion is necessary for wounding?"

This point of view is only available after you have experienced your core truth and have begun to develop your Spiritual Cosmology. All emotional wounds are self-inflicted. Some spiritual masters maintain that all wounds physical, spiritual, and emotional are self-inflicted. The foundation for this radical statement is this truth, "No one can make us think, feel, or do, anything we do not choose to think, feel, or do."

In the Spiritual Cosmology, each individual is responsible for his or her own life experience.

Looking out at the world through your cosmological screen allows you to immerse yourself in the Cultural Cosmology. In this immersed state, one can imagine almost anything as long as it supports his core issue. Emotional experiences such as guilt, rejection, abandonment, paralyzing fear, revenge, and destruction of self-worth feel real.

We physically and emotionally respond to these experiences as if they actually happen. The degree of immersion may be determined by the emotional intensity of the perceived wounding experience. In other words, emotional intensity determines the realness of the wounding experience.

The more real a wounding experience is felt, the more difficult it is to heal. As long as one remains immersed, blame and cause are often more important than healing.

While you are immersed in the Cultural Cosmology, the allure of transformation or a quick fix is more powerful than transmutation or growth.

The reality of this has led many of my clients to ask this question, "Why does it take longer to integrate the Spiritual Cosmology in some situations rather than in others?"

An answer is, while it is true, we are free to choose our interpretation of a wounding experience, immersion can make this difficult. It can be difficult for a number of reasons such as:

Confusion between pleasure and pain
The perceived wound is close to our core issue.
Timing for our own growth

Whatever the reason, the intensity of the immersion makes it difficult to withdraw to the observer perspective.

The one thing I would like you to take with you from this section of the book is the understanding that operational definitions can be more powerful in everyday life than dictionary definitions. It has been my experience that operational definitions, that emerge out of "knowings," may be difficult to communicate to others.

Communication is at times difficult between someone who has a Spiritual Cosmology and someone who has a Cosmological Screen. Definitions and concepts no longer share the same common data base.

This is why it may be easier to talk with someone who knows his core truth, than with a long time friend who does not. very true

A TOOLBOX

One of my hobbies is furniture building. I discovered over the years that although I can build a piece of furniture with simple hand tools, it is a lot easier and more efficient to use power tools, as well as other modern equipment.

When developing your Spiritual Cosmology, it is helpful to have a well stocked toolbox. What follows are a whole range of ideas, concepts and strategies that have been helpful to my clients and me. They are not organized in any particular fashion, because each one is self-contained. You will discover as you grow that this may be one of the most helpful sections of the book.

◆ Useful Concepts For Processing Rational Thoughts

Knowing a definitive definition for what is real.
This provides you with a referent for rational thinking.

Understanding what your core issue and core beliefs are.
This provides you a structure with which to view your past and present.

Substituting a new reality based statement of self-identity.
This provides you with a position by which you can compare thoughts about yourself and decide which ones you will believe.

If you know the truth, it will make you free.
If what you believe is not making you feel free, then it is not true.

define

175

Examining antithetical statements
This provides you with highly visible issues that can be resolved easily.

Being aware of self-defeating thoughts
Once you know what is real about you and have a new self-identity then self-defeating thoughts become obvious and can be changed.

◆ Strategies
For Pulling Your Awareness Of Self, Back To Living Consciously
(Back To Being Aware You Are An Observer)

There are times when you become lost. You have lost perspective and cannot see, hear, or feel from what perspective you are living. At these times it is helpful to have strategies that enable you to remember that you are always an observer, (I am not the perception; I am the perceiver) observing the world and yourself through your interpretation of your perspective.

Here are lists of strategies that might be helpful when you feel lost and confused. The most effective strategy is to remember that whatever you are feeling or experiencing will pass. Your core truth will assert itself. Knowing this from experience, you can be gentle with yourself and allow yourself to be the way you are rather than the way you should be.

❖ Going to bed

❖ Change external stimulus
 i.e. music, location, eating, making love, etc.

176

❖ Totem or symbol for self-identity

Totems are a symbol or image that some people use to represent themselves. A totem is often an animal or bird that the person identifies with. Quite often people use totems in their spiritual practices. When one is not only aware of one's totem, but has studied and interconnected with it, he knows the totem is a manifestation of the self. Thus by visualizing, talking to, or by feeling the totem, he can remember who he is.

❖ Asking questions from an I or me positions, examples are
  – Am I experiencing what I want to experience?
  – What am I thinking?
  – What am I truly certain of right now?
  – What is my body telling me right now?
  – From what position, internal, external am I seeing things right now?
  – From whose perspective am I viewing this situation?
  – Am I hearing the other person or am I hearing myself thinking?

❖ Concepts (asking questions about what concepts are currently involved)
  – Context
  – Perspective
  – Color- texture- or sound
  – Time- past, present, or future

❖ Issues of power
- Who is the source of power in this situation or circumstance?
- What is the source of power in this situation or circumstance?
- Where is the source of power in this situation or circumstance?

❖ Issues of love
- At this moment, does what I am experiencing as love, have conditions?
- If what I have labeled, as love is not love, what is it?

❖ Does my perspective of the situation promote movement or growth?

It is helpful to note that these strategies involve asking questions. A real clue for becoming aware that we are immersed in the Cultural Cosmology is the use of declarative statements for rhetorical questions.

If critically examined, these statements are usually judgmental and critical.

The use of real questions (questions that lead to answers) is in itself a powerful tool for pulling oneself out of the immersion.

The experience of asking a real question, while being immersed is like being totally involved in a good movie and someone asks us, "What is the movie about?" In order to answer the question we have to leave the world that was created by the good movie.

◆ Becoming Aware Of States Of Consciousness

Living unconsciously

> Totally immersed in the Cultural Cosmology
> Your body and mind react to thoughts out of the dynamic interplay between positions of external and internal. There is little or no awareness of the positions being separate. Example: you are unconsciously driving a car.

Reality cannot be questioned because of the sense of certainty that is experienced while being immersed in this unconscious state.

Living semiconsciously

> You are aware that there is a you and there is a there. Two distinct positions exist; therefore, a dialogue or an argument between the internal and the external can take place. Which position is right becomes important. An example would be road rage.

Reality comes to be defined through the experience of being certain about your judgment of right and wrong.

Living consciously

> You are aware of yourself and there being something out "there." The "there" is something to observe and be aware of. A distinct awareness of distance between the observer and what is being observed becomes possible.

Reality is defined and experienced by the observer

Living unconsciously in reality (living in the moment)

The concept of distinct is transmuted into the concept of unique. Distinct carries with it an implication of separateness. Unique implies special within a greater context. Unique is one of a kind. There is a self and there is an us.

Reality just is.

The tools in the toolbox are not meant to be exhaustive. As time goes by the toolbox can and will be expanded. If you develop tools that you find helpful, please share them with others. Remember reality is more complex than anyone can comprehend. Your point of view may be what I need to help me grow. There are no professionals in reality; there is only you and your perspective. I may not agree with your point of view about what we are seeing, but that does not mean I can not benefit from trying to see things from your perspective. This is how I believe conflicts can be successfully resolved and mutual growth can occur.

Helpful concepts, the next part of this lesson, are similar to the toolbox in that they have developed out of mutual exploration and conversations.

HELPFUL CONCEPTS

When building furniture it is not enough to have tools, you also have to know how to build furniture. What follows are three concepts that may be instructive as you grow in your Spiritual Cosmology.

◆ Processing Using Rational Thought

Processing means, to change an undesirable state of mind to one that is more effective or empowering.

It is difficult to accomplish this while immersed in the Cultural Cosmology and viewing the world through a cosmological screen.

For many people immersed in the Cultural Cosmology processing is unintentional or haphazard. Most people just want to feel good and are content to blame others for their state of mind.

The reasons for this are many and varied. Many do not know it is possible to think rationally; they do not think they are capable of rational processing; they believe it does not really work.

One's core issue and beliefs play a significant role in determining the use and the outcome of rational processing. If you believe that you are stupid, a victim, a loser or in some other way deficit, it will be difficult for you to have success in processing your thoughts and emotions.

Rational thoughts are thoughts that are rooted in reality rather than in imagination. They tend to be logical and internally consistent. There are tools that the mind can use to create meaningful order out of the natural confusion created by living in a complex society.

181

The key concept in rational thought is reality. The computer age has given rise to a useful concept, "garbage in, and garbage out." In other words if what you are processing is imaginary then no matter how much rational thought you use, the results will also be imaginary.

Within the Spiritual Cosmology, reality is defined as what you can photograph. If something is real then someone else can see it too. This is a helpful concept, because it forces you to examine what you are trying to process before you spend the time and energy trying to resolve it.

Rational processing does not depend so much on declarative statements as it does on penetrating questions.

Questions like "Are my results reasonable? Do they make sense? and How do I know they are true?" can be effective in evaluating the results of process.

Because the mind seeks certainty and order, rational thought can be an effective tool for changing your state of mind even if you are in the Cultural Cosmology.

It can become a profound tool when used within the context of the Spiritual Cosmology.

Becoming your core truth and developing a Spiritual Cosmology give you a position from which to process. This position can be precisely expressed in the following three statements:

- You are not the thought; you are the thinker.
- You are not the perception; you are that which perceives.
- You are not the emotion; you are that which experiences the emotion.

Addicted to Certainty

The Cultural Cosmology in general and the cosmological screen specifically, create the illusion that we are what we think, perceive, or feel. The magic of the illusion is a consequence of becoming immersed through our screen in the Cultural Cosmology.

Within the Spiritual Cosmology, the definition of reality undergoes a profound change. One no longer defines reality as that which he sincerely believes, but rather it is defined by what he knows and experiences. One of the most profound things he knows and experiences is that, he is not the perception, rather he is that which perceives.

"Garbage in" or things that are imaginary are easily spotted when viewed from a Spiritual Cosmology. As one comes to more clearly identify and understand one's core beliefs and ultimately one's core issue, antithetical statements and self-defeating patterns become very evident.

This is especially true when we have broken the bonds of false certainty that bind us to our core issue.

Out of the experience of knowing that, the only thing that is certain is that you exist, the mind begins to reorder itself. With this new, experiential definition of reality, the mind reassesses old beliefs and definitions and begins to discards those that no longer work.

Processing, using rational thought, becomes a familiar and comfortable tool that enables us to change our state of mind from a Cultural Cosmology to a Spiritual Cosmology.

E. Jack Lemon

◆ Knowing The Relationship Between Certainty, Truth, And Reality

In order to examine any relationship, one must have a clear definition of the participants in the relationship.

In order to have a clear definition one must determine whether one is talking about a vocabulary definition or an operational definition.

A vocabulary definition is one that can be found in a dictionary. Our culture has given to academicians and grammarians the power to define words precisely. These precise definitions are the tools, which are fundamentally necessary for clear communication.

An operational definition is one that grows out of an individual's experience. This kind of definition tends to be personal, contextual, and imprecise. It is because it is personal and contextual, that it has great power over how we communicate with ourselves. This imprecision is irrelevant in our conversations with ourselves.

The reason for this is that people respond both consciously and unconsciously to their own familiar meanings of concepts rather than the objective meanings given by academicians.

The process that we use for creating an operational definition of a concept is similar to the process that we use for creating a belief:

- We first make the association between a concept and its meaning or behavior.
- If this association seems to work for us, we use it again.
- As we reassess and find that the association continues to work, it becomes familiar and feels comfortable and natural.

- The longer we use the association, the more we believe it and feel confidence in it.
- The longer we have confidence in the association, the more we believe and experience it to be true.
- At some point in this process, the association between a concept and its meaning or behavior moves from just being true to our experiencing it as fact.
- We are now feeling quite certain that our definition is real.

Now when we experience our definition, we believe it, regardless of what academicians or other people say. We hold to this belief even if our mind offers a different point of view. This is how bigotry, racism, homophobia, and class definitions are created.

Certainty is the feeling that we experience when we believe something is true. This feeling becomes deeper, stronger, or clearer when we know with certainty something is real.

Each person experiences the association between certainty and truth, and certainty and reality differently.

The reason that this feeling of certainty is associated with truth and reality is that it provides the brain with two important and valued functions: the feeling of certainty is an organizing principle for the brain as it seeks order out of confusion, and it provides the body/mind a criterion for making itself safe.

It is helpful to note that because the associational process occurs in the milieu of living, the mind is only interested in whether the association works. It is not interested in whether the association is accurate or helpful.

When one has a new "I-am" statement as a result of experiencing I exist because I am aware of my thinking, this new association is made rationally and

E. Jack Lemon

quickly because it is now rooted and associated with the experience of being certain of what is real.

This new foundational statement of identity has immediate power and will grow in its power as time goes on.   Your mind will begin to respond to the resulting confusion of a change of identity.   It will respond by recreating your cosmological screen in light of this new definition of certainty and reality.

You will notice this recreating process when your thoughts and behavior change naturally from self defeating to self-empowering.

◆ Criteria For Decision Making

How can one be confident about his choices when he is using, "What do I believe is real?" rather than "What is right or wrong?"

The key word in this question is confident. The reason it is key is that it connotes a cosmology that is nondeterministic. If the word "certain" were substituted for confident the meaning of the question would be quite different.

In reality, we cannot know the outcome of any decision for certain. This truism is reflected in the scientific method where one hypothesizes, experiments, and evaluates. The scientific method is rooted in the assumption that something cannot ever be known for fact; it can only be proven accurate thus far.

We are called on to make decisions about a myriad of things everyday. We are not usually comfortable guessing at how we should answer these questions because guessing feels like blind chance.

We would like to make decisions knowing for certain our choice is right. The problem with this is, in order for the choice to be right, we have to know all of the consequences for our decision. We would then be able to choose the specific consequence that would work.

Personal, as well as social experiences, teach us that every decision has many unintended outcomes. These unintended consequences often reveal to us that a better decision could have been made if we had more information.

The emotional response to making a wrong decision is often to feel inadequate, embarrassed or dumb. This emotional response also leads us to have less confidence in ourselves and our ability to make good decisions.

E. Jack Lemon

We often tell ourselves, "I should learn from my failure"; however, we still have emotionally experienced ourselves as failing. The body/mind's response to failure is not a helpful experience, because it reinforces our negative core beliefs and issue.

If guessing is not desirable and certainty is not possible, then there must be a basis for decision-making that lies in between these two extremes.

> I would suggest that two of these would be
> *"What do I believe is real?"* and *"Reasonableness."*

These two concepts give me a foundation to make everyday decisions. They are concepts that I can use and be loyal to. Loyalty means allegiance to something.

Since it is not possible to have allegiance to certainty regarding the future, then allegiance to principles, you believe to be real and reasonable, seem the most appropriate. In the Spiritual Cosmology, we know that these principles are evolving. This evolution occurs naturally, as we grow in age and in experience.

Using allegiance to one's principles implies a certain degree of ongoing awareness of these principles. One of the consequences of developing a Spiritual Cosmology is that one not only is aware of these principles, but one is also vigorously evaluating them, using what *works for me* as criteria for this evaluation.

Once one knows the principles out of which he will make a decision, he is free to ask non-judgmental questions. Example of these would be, "What is reasonable in this situation? " and "How do I know what I am experiencing is real?"

188

This question of reasonableness carries with it the implication of what is the best alternative I have, given my knowledge of the situation. This implication naturally leads one to assess the outcome of the decision, without fear of judgment. The evaluation of the decision is conducted within the framework of growth.

The question, "What do I know is real in this situation?" leads to my core truth and my knowings. It especially leads one to the fact, "That no one can make me think, feel, or do, anything I do not choose to think, feel, or do."

Questions that naturally emerge out of a framework of growth could be

Are the results what I expected?
What factors affected the outcome?
What decision would have been more appropriate?

* Note that none of these questions is judgmental or create condemnation.

When one is making decisions out of a Spiritual Cosmology, he develops confidence in his ability to make decisions rather than having to be confident that a specific decision is right. This confidence leads to a more effective decision-making ability.

This more effective decision-making ability leads to a life style that is rooted in growth, rather than in fear.

These are just a few of the concepts that have undergone a change in meaning because of going to "that place." You will discover that your familiar concepts will undergo a similar redefinitional process.

E. Jack Lemon

The last section of the book is about the implication of the Spiritual Cosmology. These are personal observations and conclusions. In many ways, it is a rational "map" of my journey thus far.

It has been my observation that anyone who has been to "that place" and experienced his core truth will be open to spiritual exploration.

What I believe thus far

"The more one grows to know oneself
the more one can grow to know
God and the world"

Is there a God?

Cosmological assumption- there is a perceived order in the universe and there is no ability to predict the future except in probabilities.

Since there is an order in reality (without predictability), is there an organizing principle that I can come to understand and respond to?

One is free to ask and explore this question when there is no over riding morality against it., specifically a morality that demands absolutes and searches for certainty.

Spiritual Cosmology promotes questions rather than dogmatic answers.

In searching new territory, it is often helpful to see if anyone has gone there before you.

Regarding the specific question, religion is a helpful place to start. It is particularly helpful to rule out any religious positions that have absolute values embedded in their teachings.

In fact it may be the most helpful to study the lives of the primary teachers of any religion before examining what people say are their teachings.

It is also important to explore our own experience, because we only truly believe and feel certain about what we experience ourselves.

One other source of information that would be helpful is the stories and experiences of people we trust.

E. Jack Lemon

Based on my exploration and study of all the above, exploring my own experience, searching for knowledge from spiritual teachers and their writings and the stories and experiences of trusted people, I find that it is reasonable to assume that there is an organizing principle to creation.

What would be the attributes of such an organizing principle?

It is easiest to describe what they could not be.

The organizing principle could not be absolute, judgmental, guilt producing, moral, in an objective sense, or controlling.

It also would not contradict what I experience and perceive in creation since by implication, it would be the creator, as well as the organizing principle. It, however, could and by definition would be more than what I experience and perceive in creation.

It would affirm observed reality as opposed to cultural reality.

Because of what I know of the experience of Jesus, Buddha, people I trust, and my own experience, I believe that this organizing principle would wish to communicate and facilitate my knowledge of it.

It is clear that from a Spiritual Cosmology perspective this process would occur most efficiently when one is experiencing the present, since by definition this organizing principle could not exist in my memories of the past or in my anticipation of the future.

The one thing that all of the above sources seems to imply, infer, and/or declare is that the organizing principle would be unconditional love.

Unconditional love is an acceptance of what is, at any given moment, without a comparison or judgment.

192

a state of Being, of awesome wonder

It is my experience that it is a healing energy urging creation to grow. It does not need our adoration or obedience, yet rejoices in our journey toward becoming present in unconditional love.

Also my experience informs me that the more I develop my Spiritual Cosmology, the more self-evident it becomes, there is a natural relationship between whatever I call the Creator and me.

This relationship is available for me to expand and explore. I do this with the realization that a natural consequence of this expansion is that I can be transmuted into the experience of unconditional love.

As an ordained Presbyterian minister, I know this transmutation is possible because of the life and teachings of Jesus Christ. I also know that the creator is active in this transmutation because of the experience of the Resurrection and Pentecost.

In addition, my studies and experience with the Native American Pipe, as well as my experience with Buddhism, confirm this realization.

Experiencing self as awareness

The self does not exist as a place or an event but rather as the present, a moment in time. Because I am living in space and time, I can imagine I am connected to the past through memory and the future through anticipation.

The cultural mind defines the self as if it were a substance, separate and distinct from the universe.

However, any sense of separation is an illusion created by the mind, but is, nonetheless, a necessary part of the journey from awakening at birth to self-realization.

E. Jack Lemon

The self is on a journey whether it acknowledges it
or not. The teacher imbedded in the journey is experience. We still, like our ancient fore parents, use "what
works" in our experience as a mechanism by which we
grow.

The amazing thing about this mechanism of using,
what *works for us*, is that it is so flexible that as we grow
and our perspective changes, the mechanism continues to
work effectively. We choose "what works" and discard
what does not.

The journey of self-knowledge has moved us from
the dim awakening of ourselves as merely separate from
the world, to embracing the external world as "we" or
tribal.

In time, we move to see ourselves as a distinct part
of the tribe, not just us as the tribe.

From this position, we begin to challenge the
presuppositions of the tribe and grow to make choices
different from and distinct from the tribe.

There does come a point when the self decides
that its perspective is more important than that of the
tribe or culture.

This is the jumping off point when the self begins
to create its own reality and explores the illusion of a
deterministic certainty.

From this new point of view, the self becomes the
one who can choose what is real and possible.

If we believe the spiritual teachers, it is possible
from this position to experience nature, body awareness,
time, and reality from a point of view that is different
from the deterministic perspective. It is, however, so
different from the deterministic perspective that it may
not be communicable to others who have not had similar
experiences.

It is from this perspective that one begins to believe it is truly possible to experience the present as all there is.

This experience of being fully present can be truly life changing, because in that moment there is no sense of separation. There is only room for the awareness of all things and your place in it.

This experience, the duration of which is entirely personal, provides you with the necessary foundational understanding to facilitate the process of growth into a truly Spiritual Cosmology.

Everything the self knows and believes is filtered through a cosmological screen. This screen organizes information, decides what to keep and how it will be organized. It tells us what is possible and what is real, as well as what to trust and what to fear. It creates definitions and values, which the self acts on as it experiences life.

One way to describe the self's growth is to say growth is the modifying of our cosmological screen.

As our screen is altered, whether by ourselves, through our interpretations of personal experiences, or through accepting the interpretations of others, we change.

This altering of our cosmological screen, which is accomplished by discovering, "what works" for us through experience, affects our perspective of God, ourselves, other people, and things in our world.

We cannot know God, the world, or ourselves in any total or absolute sense, because what we know depends on our perspective. When we truly experience the certainty of this, we are free to explore and experience as much of God, the world, and ourselves as we choose.

We are also free to explore our past and discover how we have grown rather than to judge how bad/wrong others or we were. We are free to discover our core beliefs, and ultimately our core issue, which are the foundational structures of our screen and to change them.

This will naturally lead us to be healed of our self-inflicted wounds. This healing of our old wounds by changing our core issue and recognizing how we have grown from our mistakes rather than being judged by them makes possible the deep healing or letting go of the past.

This experience of deep healing can be called forgiving ourselves, but when we experience the present, we discover that there is nothing to forgive.

We can then also allow others to come to their own conclusions about themselves, Spirit, and the world.

It is out of allowing for this diversity of conclusions that a new kind of community can and will naturally emerge.

This community is one that communicates, shares, supports, challenges, and rejoices with each other's process and journey, rather than needing to evaluate and validate the conclusion of the journey.

This community exists and continues to grow in its practice.

After Word

The more I grow in experience the more I understand the limitless depths of Mitakuye oyas'in (all are my relatives).

I was asked once, "Who were the people and ideas that influenced me?" How do I answer such a question? The assumptions implicit in it are conflicted. The question assumes a linear understanding of time. It also assumes that there is a me that has been influenced. This is a me that has existed since March 13, 1948, and is just being modified as I grow. That person does not exist except in my memory and in the memories of those who knew me.

I share this with you to illustrate how difficult it can be to answer seemly simple questions that originate from a different cosmology from your own.

I was told yesterday by someone whom I respect, that it is proper to acknowledge those with whom we are connected. Because of my respect and love for this person, I will try to do so.

If I were to acknowledge and give thanks for the threads in my blanket of life, I would start with the loving energy of Spirit, that I call "Grandfather." I would also bear witness to Jesus, whom I call, the Christ, and the Buddha. Other strands would be the profound experiences of Communion, Pipe Ceremonies, and celebrations in worship and at sweat lodges at Bear Creek Farm.

Regarding people, who could I lift up as most special: my teachers, my friends, my enemies, the checkout lady who gave me a smile when I needed it, my grandchild Everet, my son Christopher?

E. Jack Lemon

At what time in life, do I separate out and say this is who I was and this was the influence on me?

Let me simple say, that I am who I am at this moment, because of my interactions with all aspects of the universe. If you have known me during my life please receive my gratitude and this blessing, Peace and "Namaste" (I see the universe and myself reflected in you).

Jack
Bear Creek Farm 2/5/2006

The Glossary

Absolute
Something that is true in all cases. It is a fact and has no exceptions. In the Cultural Cosmology, many things are believed or felt to be absolutes, but are in fact contextual i.e. Ten Commandments, truth, and your core issue.
In the Spiritual Cosmology, the only absolutes are

You are aware that you exist.
You are thinking; therefore, you exist.
All that exists is everything, in the present moment.

Addiction
Addiction is when you are unable to control your interaction with something.

Antithetical Or Contradictory Statements
Antithetical statements are two statements that are exactly the opposite of each other. Example: one can believe that, "You should look before you leap" and one also can believe that, "He who hesitates is lost." If someone has both of these beliefs at the same time, his only real choice is to do nothing.

Authentic Self
The authentic self is the experience of the self as uniquely existing in the world. It is the state into which we were born. It is not dependent on anything else for its existence at any give moment. The experience of the authentic self is the experience that we are.

Blame

Blame is to fix or establish responsibility for an action. This can be a person, situation, or anything one can imagine existing outside of himself. When one is immersed in the Cultural Cosmology, blame is very important. It is how we avoid responsibility and being wrong. From the perspective of the Spiritual Cosmology we know that no one can make us think, feel, or do anything, we do not choose to think, feel, or do. There is literally no one you can blame for anything that you experience except yourself. Since the overall structure of the Spiritual Cosmology is growth, judging or blaming yourself is pointless. It is much more efficient to evaluate your behavior and discover how you could act differently in the future.

Certainty

Certainty is a sense that is experienced by the mind through the body when we feel something is true. How this sense is experienced is highly individual. It may be experienced as something being clearer, more solid or just feels right.

Cognitive Dissonance

Cognitive dissonance is experienced as a feeling of discomfort when the mind becomes aware of antithetical or contradictory statements about reality. This feeling of unease and confusion is a necessary experience when one is trying to drain the sense of certainty from a particular point of awareness. It is through this process that one can reach "that place."

Consequences

Consequences are intended and unintended outcomes from a specific decision or action taken. Consequences occur whether one's perspective is Cultural Cosmology or Spiritual Cosmology. The difference is in the interpretation of the meaning given to an action and its outcome.

Core Beliefs

Core beliefs are a loosely allied network of beliefs that emerge out of and support the core issue. They share a similar degree of certainty with the core issue. These beliefs are created in the same way that all beliefs are created.

– You make an association between an interpretation of an event and the event.
– If this happens a number of times and the interpretation seems correct, you believe it.
– If you believe the interpretation is correct long enough then, it becomes truth.
– If you experience the interpretation as truth long enough, it becomes fact and, therefore, certain.

Beliefs are at their essence a habitual way of thinking that feels true. When simple beliefs become core beliefs, they provide the structural girders for the cosmological screen. They become the structures that make up our interpretation of reality. Core beliefs are essentially habitual patterns. These patterns allow a person, especially with the help of a therapist, to identify specific core beliefs. Because they share a similar degree of certainty with the core issue, a system of interconnected core beliefs is very resistant to therapeutic intervention. Therapy may be successful in helping the person redefine a specific core belief, but it has been my experience that

over time the specific belief is reinterpreted in such a fashion that it continues to support the other core beliefs and ultimately the hidden core issue.

Core Issue

Simply put our core issue is the conclusional statement of self-identity that each one of us makes to ourselves somewhere between the ages of two and five. This conclusional identity statement is the product of socializing with parents, siblings, and others. The undeveloped mind actively seeks an organizing principle. This is a principle that will enable the child to sort out who he is and what his relationship to the greater world is. Because this search for an organizing principle takes place at the same time that parents are trying to socialize the child, the core issue usually is expressed in negative terms. The context of the core issue might be overtly social such as: I am not good enough or I am not wanted. It can also be intrapersonal within a social context such as: I should not exist or I am an accident. Whatever the context, this conclusional statement provides the framework out of which a child will interpret his place in the world. Since this conclusion is one that he derived on his own from data that he himself gathered, and additionally since there was no one in his world that could read his mind and intervene with an alternative perspective, this conclusion is as close to certain truth as there is. Because of the high degree of certainty associated with this conclusional statement of self-identity, and because it occurred at a very early age, it is difficult to identify it by yourself. It is also highly resistant to therapeutic intervention, because it is hidden and perceived as truth.

Core Truth

The core truth is an identity statement that emerges out of the experience of doubting everything that exists, except that you are aware you are thinking. The core truth is not so much a declarative statement as it is a description of who you have discovered yourself to be. It is not the opposite of your core issue nor does it heal your core issue in any obvious sense. The experience of recognizing your core truth makes your core issue impossible. The certainty of your core truth drains away your certainty of the core issues and core beliefs. This dissolving of the sense of certainty about your core issue and core beliefs allows your mind to restructure your experience of reality. This restructuring is based now on a truth that is self-evident and not dependent on social validation.

Cosmological Screen

The Cosmological Screen is the interpretive filter through which we experience our lives. In the Cultural Cosmology, the cosmological screen is framed by our core issue and webbed by our core beliefs. In many ways, our cosmological screen mirrors the Cultural Cosmology. It believes that reality is knowable, predictable, and controllable. It also believes that the memories of the past are accurate and its anxieties about the future are appropriate. Our cosmological screen knows that cause-and-effect exist and that most the time failure is our fault.

Cosmology

Cosmology is a theory or belief about the nature of the world. Examples of cosmological questions are "What is the world?" and "How does it operate?"

Cultural Cosmology

Cultural Cosmology is the sum total of the mores, beliefs and laws that enable a group to live together successfully. This point of view must have as its cosmological assumptions that reality is knowable, predictable, and controllable. The relationship between one's cosmological screen and Cultural Cosmology is so interdependent that the existence of a Cultural Cosmology is virtually unknown.

Cultural Reality (See Cultural Cosmology)

Cultural reality is the perceived experience of living in a society.

Deterministic Reality

Deterministic reality believes that the past determines the future. It believes reality is knowable, predictable, and controllable. Linearity is an important concept in deterministic thinking.

Discipline

Discipline means the ability to act in a consistent, but not in a fixed or rigid fashion. This ability is developed out of the experience of growth rather than imposed by will or culture. Discipline in this context is a process not a determined strategy.

Emotional Bog

When we are fully associated or immersed in the Cultural Cosmology, it is easy for us to believe that life situations involving strong emotions, cause and effect, blame and guilt are natural and normal. One of the unintended outcomes of developing a Spiritual Cosmology is that these beliefs feel strange and unnatural. One of my clients describes this experience as being in a murky bog, a place where everything feels shaky and you want solid footing. This emotional experience is a clear indication of a developing Spiritual Cosmology. Having a Spiritual Cosmology allows your mind to have a solid place on which to stand. Even though the Cultural Cosmology says the situations of strong emotion, blame, and guilt are real, the mind no longer believes it. This conflict can leave you feeling like you are up to your neck in an emotional bog.

Immersion

The concept of immersion only makes sense after one has experienced the reality of "that place." Once you have experienced being in "that place "and know beyond any possibility of doubt that you exist, it is difficult to believe that the Cultural Cosmology is real. That is not to say that you cannot forget who you are and become totally associated with the Cultural Cosmology. A person can and does experience this association or immersion; however, one can at any moment remember who he really is and once again observe the Cultural Cosmology rather than being in it. One of the most powerful indicators of the state of immersion is strong negative emotion. This is what one experiences as the emotional bog. Other easily identified indicators of immersion are the use of blame language and parental imperatives such as must, have to, and should. The power of immersion wanes as the cosmological screen transmutes into the core truth and its knowings. Pulling oneself back out of the immersion is often described as waking from a dream. In a very real way, it is an accurate description of what the Cultural Cosmology and the cosmological screen really are. They are dream states that must be believed in sincerely in order for them to be perceived as real.

Individual-Consciousness Cosmology

Individual-consciousness cosmology is a personal perspective of the nature of the world, rather than a social perspective. It assumes there is an individual aspect of consciousness that questions, explores, creates, and ultimately seeks to become self-aware.

Linearity

Linearity is a perspective of reality based on a belief in the direct relationship between cause and effect. Linearity assumes that one can know the cause of something and the corresponding effect, as separate entities that have a specific interconnected relationship. Linearity is a necessary component of the Cultural Cosmology. Because of it, one can fix blame for a behavior, as well as render judgment.

Memory

Memory is a function of the mind that enables a person to view the past. Within the Cultural Cosmology, memory is assumed to be an accurate representation of the past. The Spiritual Cosmology realizes that a memory is a highly edited version of a specific interpretation of a possible past event. A memory is not only an edited interpretation, it is an interpretation from a specific point of view and context. Memory within the Spiritual Cosmology is not a representation of reality.

Observed Reality

Observed reality is simply our perceptions of the world and ourselves. Observed reality may include the interpretations of our perceptions, but there is a clear distinction between perception and interpretation.

Observer

While being immersed in the Cultural Cosmology, one is unaware of the distinction between perception and reality. Perception is our interpretation of what exists. Reality is what exists in any given moment. While in the Cultural Cosmology, we believe our perception of reality is true and accurate. When we have a Spiritual Cosmology, we are aware that reality exists and that we are a part of it. Because of our self-awareness we are able to observe ourselves relating to the world without judgment. This unique point of view is called the observer. From this perspective we know:

> I am not the thought; I am the thinker
> I am not the perception; I am the perceiver
> I am not the emotion; I am experiencing the emotion

Reality

Subjective Reality - is what we sincerely believe is real
Personal Reality - the knowing that results from
> experiencing your own existence
Greater Reality - all that exists in the moment

Responsibility

Responsibility is what one will be held accountable for. There is an assumed relationship between a person and what he feels accountable for. While being immersed in the Cultural Cosmology, one can be held accountable for almost anything, even if he did not agree to it. The Spiritual Cosmological perspective is that one is accountable for himself and his perspectives. There are obligations that a person with a Spiritual Cosmological perspective will agree to; however, only he can hold himself accountable for the consequences of his actions.

The reason for this is that a person with a Spiritual Cosmological perspective knows that cause and effect cannot be known with certainty; therefore, accountability is based on his interpretation and context of the situation, rather than on some objective point of view. A person with a Spiritual Cosmology can decide to drive 50 miles an hour in a twenty mile an hour zone. When he is stopped, he will not blame anyone other than himself for his ticket.

Self

The Cultural Cosmology defines the self as if it were a substance, separate and distinct from the universe. The Spiritual Cosmology explains that the self does not exist as a place or an event but rather as the present, a moment in time, connected to the past only through memory and to the future only through anticipation. The self within this context ultimately knows only two things for certain; it is thinking; therefore, it exists, and everything else that exists in the universe exists only in the moment.

Spiritual

Spiritual is when a person out of the realness that he truly is, relates to the universe that is also real. This dynamic interaction is my definition for being spiritual. Whatever labels I have for the Creator, its creation and its interaction with me as part of creation, are just symbols. These symbols vaguely refer to what is essentially an uncommunicatable experience. It is especially uncommunicatable to a person who does not know his core truth. This is not to say that I do not try to communicate my experience with others, and try to understand theirs.

Mitakuye oyas'in (all are my relatives) is not a cute saying; it is the reality of life, what I specifically experience in my interaction with the Creator is uniquely my own. Even the experience of love, that can exist between God, others and me as in celebrations, is still the experience of my interpretation of my perception.

Spiritual Cosmology

Spiritual Cosmology describes reality as being much more complex than we can comprehend. This complexity cannot be comprehended totally. Because we are a part of it, we, therefore, are influenced by it. As a result, anything we know about reality is our personal interpretation, except for the fact that we are aware we exist. With this as a foundation, one is able to experience his life without the paralysis of judgment, absolutes, overwhelming guilt, and unreasonable anger. One can live his life out of the freedom that comes from having the power to make choices and learning from the consequences. The Spiritual Cosmology is a perspective where the past and future are basically imaginary and the only thing that exists in time and space has existence in the moment. This perspective is antithetical to the Cultural Cosmology, which believes that reality is knowable, predictable, and controllable, as well as believing passionately in the existence of past and future.

Transmutation

Transmutation is a change that occurs gradually and in an interconnected fashion. Another word for transmutation is growth. This is dramatically different from transformation. Transformation is an abrupt change that may not have any connection to a previous condition. Another word for transformation is conversion.

The growth from a Cultural Cosmology to a Spiritual Cosmology is necessarily transmutation because it involves the restructuring of how we perceive reality and ourselves. This restructuring is so fundamental that if it occurred abruptly, it would affect the mental and physical well being of an individual.

Index

absolute 44, 45, 46, 47, 48, 50, 55, 67, 78, 91, 92, 103, 104, 107, 108, 115, 127, 144, 149, 156, 170, 191, 192, 195, 199

addiction 22, 23, 53, 199

antithetical 26, 47, 49, 78, 164, 165, 176, 183, 199, 200, 209

authentic self 77, 78, 199

blame 57, 83, 86, 148, 149, 173, 181, 200, 204, 205, 206, 208

certainty 1, 3, 16, 21, 22, 23, 36, 44, 46, 47, 48, 57, 58, 59, 60, 61, 65, 66, 67, 68, 69, 70, 71, 72, 74, 78, 93, 98, 100, 101, 103, 104, 106, 107, 108, 109, 114, 115, 122, 125, 127, 134, 143, 144, 151, 158, 171, 179, 182, 183, 184, 185, 186, 188, 191, 194, 195, 200, 201, 202, 203, 208, 215

cognitive dissonance 26, 104, 110, 111, 115, 125, 127, 200

consequences 34, 57, 70, 72, 96, 144, 151, 168, 187, 188, 201, 207, 209

core beliefs 45, 67, 79, 85, 87, 88, 89, 92, 93, 94, 95, 96, 97, 102, 107, 117, 134, 153, 154, 155, 165, 175, 183, 188, 196, 201, 202, 203

core issue 45, 67, 75, 79, 85, 86, 87, 88, 89, 90, 91, 92, 93, 94, 95, 96, 97, 98, 99, 100, 101, 102, 103, 104, 107, 117, 123, 125, 126, 134, 135, 136, 153, 154, 155, 161, 171, 172, 173, 174, 175, 181, 183, 196, 199, 201, 202, 203

core truth 6, 79, 86, 87, 92, 98, 99, 100, 101, 102, 103, 104, 108, 123, 125, 126, 127, 128, 129, 130, 133, 134, 136, 137, 138, 139, 141, 154, 155, 161, 172, 173, 174, 176, 182, 189, 190, 203, 205, 208

cosmological screen 42, 45, 50, 54, 57, 58, 65, 66, 76, 77, 78, 81, 85, 86, 87, 89, 90, 92, 98, 104, 107, 111, 115, 117, 119, 120, 121, 125, 126, 131, 133, 136, 137, 141, 144, 153, 154, 172, 173, 174, 181, 183, 186, 195, 201, 203, 204, 205, 215

cosmology 3, 26, 46, 47, 48, 49, 52, 53, 54, 55, 56, 57, 58, 74, 76, 79, 81,
85, 87, 125, 131, 133, 134, 135, 136, 137, 138, 139, 141, 142, 143, 144,
146, 147, 148, 149, 150, 152, 156, 157, 158, 159, 160, 161, 162, 165,
166, 167, 168, 169, 170, 171, 173, 174, 175, 178, 179, 181, 182, 183,
187, 188, 189, 190, 191, 192, 193, 195, 197, 199, 200, 201, 203, 204,
205, 206, 207, 208, 209, 210, 215

cultural cosmology 3, 46, 48, 49, 52, 53, 55, 57, 79, 81, 85, 87, 133,
135, 139, 141, 143, 146, 147, 148, 157, 160, 162, 166, 167, 168, 169,
170, 171, 173, 178, 179, 181, 182, 183, 199, 200, 201, 203, 204, 205,
206, 207, 208, 209, 210, 215

deterministic reality 46, 57, 78, 79, 204

discipline 26, 57, 204

Edward 61, 62, 63, 70, 71, 74, 75, 80, 82, 85, 87, 94, 95, 97, 102, 127,
128, 130, 136, 137

Elizabeth 61, 62, 63, 70, 72, 74, 76, 80, 84, 85, 87, 94, 96, 97, 102, 103,
127, 129, 130, 136, 137

emotional bog 87, 135, 150, 151, 171, 172, 204, 205

immersion 108, 112, 113, 114, 115, 117, 173, 174, 178, 205

linearity 50, 51, 204, 206

memory 23, 68, 105, 106, 112, 146, 147, 148, 149, 160, 163, 166, 193,
197, 206, 208

observed reality 192, 206

observer 171, 174, 176, 179, 207

reality 6, 11, 13, 14, 15, 20, 23, 25, 26, 27, 33, 34, 36, 37, 42, 43, 45, 46,
47, 48, 49, 50, 52, 53, 54, 55, 57, 60, 70, 77, 78, 79, 80, 81, 85, 87, 91,
92, 104, 106, 107, 108, 111, 115, 116, 117, 118, 120, 121, 122, 133, 135,
141, 142, 149, 150, 152, 155, 158, 159, 163, 165, 166, 167, 168, 170,
172, 174, 175, 179, 180, 181, 182, 183, 184, 185, 186, 187, 191, 192,
194, 200, 201, 203, 204, 205, 206, 207, 209, 210

Seminars

Why seminars are valuable.
If you picked up this book, you may feel like you are a "stranger in a strange land." You may wonder if there is anyone else who feels the same separation that you do. By attending a seminar, you receive in-depth exploration of concepts and techniques, answers to questions, as well as the affirmation that you are not alone. The Cultural Cosmology is real and pervasive; your cosmological screen is ever present. Knowing who you truly are and always have been is empowering, even if you are all alone. However, experiencing that other people like you are responding to the yearning to "return home" is even more comforting.

If you are interested in attending or sponsoring a seminar please feel free to contact me:

E. Jack Lemon
Bear Creek Farm
9501 Dundee/Azalia Road
Maybee, Michigan 48159
www.addictedtocertainty.com

Vibrational Energy Painting

If you are interested in acquiring prints of the cover painting, wish to see other examples of Joyce's artwork or inquire about having a personal Vibrational Energy Painting done contact the artist:

Joyce Staelgraeve
Many Forks Retreat Center
8226 North Stoney Creek Road
Newport, Michigan 48166

ISBN 141209036-9